J. K. LASSER'S

ALL YOU SHOULD KNOW ABOUT IRA, KEOGH, AND OTHER RETIREMENT PLANS

By the
*J.K. Lasser
Tax Institute*

Bernard Greisman,
Editor

A FIRESIDE BOOK | *Published by*
Simon and Schuster, New York

Designed by Irving Perkins Associates

Manufactured in the United States of America

10 9 8 7 6 5 4 3 2 1

Library of Congress Cataloging in Publication Data

ISBN: 0–671–45978–3

PREFACE

THE tax laws offer incentives to save for retirement by providing benefits to individuals and businesses when they set aside money in pension plans. Whether you are an employer, employee, or are self-employed, J. K. Lasser's *All You Should Know About IRA, Keogh, and Other Retirement Plans* details options for retirement investments and shows you how to take advantage of the tax breaks allowed by law.

To live comfortably during your retirement years, you must start planning early to achieve adequate financial resources. Try to choose the type of funding which you can afford and which will meet your goals. This unique new book defines your pension alternatives and examines planning techniques which will yield the maximum tax benefits. You will find expert discussions on everything you need to know about reviewing retirement investment choices; setting up an IRA or Keogh plan; establishing an SEP for your small business or using corporate retirement plans; deciding when and how to take distributions from your plan for maximum benefits; avoiding IRA and Keogh tax penalties; keeping records for your retirement investments; your Social Security benefits; and estate planning for your retirement benefits. This authoritative guide will help you make informed decisions about how, when, and where to save for a secure retirement.

We gratefully acknowledge the contributions of Barbara E. Weltman and Elliott Eiss, members of the New York Bar, and of Helen O'Donnell, Joyce Clarke, and Linda L. Seymour, in the preparation of this book.

Bernard Greisman

CONTENTS

beneficiary, 117   Securities received as distribution, 119   How annuity payments are taxed, 121   Three-year recovery of cost, 121   How annuities are taxed if you cannot use the three-year rule, 123   How Civil Service retirement pay is taxed, 126   How beneficiaries of deceased employees report annuity payments, 127   Military personnel allowed tax exclusion on annuity election, 128   Are your retirement benefits protected from the claims of creditors and ex-spouses?, 129   Withholding tax on pension benefits, 131

9. TAX-FREE ROLLOVERS   132

Is a rollover advisable when you retire?, 132   Rules for making a tax-free rollover into an IRA or a qualified plan, 134   Changing a rollover election, 136   Rollover of proceeds from sale of property received in lump-sum distribution, 137   Rollovers of IRAs, 137   Tax-free transfer of an IRA because of divorce, 138

10. SOCIAL SECURITY   139

Qualifying for benefits, 139   Applying for Social Security retirement benefits, 142   Payment of benefits, 143   Estimating retirement benefits, 143   Social Security and retirement planning, 144   Medicare and additional health insurance, 146   Medicare coverage, 147   Benefit period, 148   Filing claims, 149   What Medicare does not cover, 149

11. ESTATE PLANNING FOR RETIREMENT
BENEFITS   151

How benefits from qualified plans are taxed, 151   Should a beneficiary elect to forgo ten-year averaging?, 153   Individual retirement plans (IRAs), 154   How death benefits under nonqualified plans are taxed, 155   Treatment of special retirement benefits, 156

Chapter 1
HIGHLIGHTS OF
THE NEW PENSION LAW

WHETHER you are an owner, an executive, or an employee, you should be concerned about pension benefits to ensure a comfortable retirement. There are several sources of retirement benefits. Your company may provide a pension when you retire. You may save through your own individual retirement account (IRA) as a primary or supplementary source of retirement dollars. You may also be entitled to Social Security and other government benefits. The chapters in this book are designed to explain each type of pension option and related investment opportunity. At the same time, you should be aware that many pension plans will undergo revisions to meet the changes made by the 1982 Tax Equity and Fiscal Responsibility Act.

Presently, the type of pension plan you select is determined in part by the way your business is organized. If your business is incorporated, you must follow the rules for qualified corporate retirement plans. If your business is unincorporated, you must follow rules for self-employed retirement plans, called Keogh plans. Currently, Keogh plans are subject to lower contribution and benefit limits and more restrictions than corporate plans. However, when the new laws become effective over the next few years, the type of business organization will no longer affect your pension plan option. Whether you are self-employed or have incorporated, retirement plans will have to meet the same basic requirements. These changes will also remove pension incentives for organizing professional incorporations. Here is a review of the important changes made by the new law.

Individual retirement plans (IRAs)

All workers may set up personal retirement plans. Contributions are tax deductible and earnings on contributions accumulate tax free. Present limits on contributions have not been changed by the new law.

Individuals with IRAs who wish to change investment vehicles may do so without tax if certain rules are observed. The change must be completed within 60 days of receiving the distribution from the present IRA. Currently, tax-free treatment is available only if the entire IRA is distributed and transferred, that is, "rolled over" to the new IRA. Beginning in 1982 partial rollovers will enjoy tax-free treatment. The portion not rolled over will be taxable.

 ## Self-employed retirement plans

If you are a sole owner or partner in an unincorporated business, you may already have a Keogh plan. These plans are subject to many restrictions not applied to corporate plans, the severest of which limits contributions and benefits for owners. The new law has eliminated these special restrictions so that, after 1983, owners of unincorporated businesses have the same pension opportunities as corporate owner-employees.

In 1982 and 1983 the maximum deduction for a Keogh profit-sharing plan is the lesser of $15,000 or 15% of earned income. In 1984 the maximum contribution limit is the same as for corporate profit-sharing plans: the lesser of 25% of earned income or $30,000.

Meeting new rules for existing plans

If you are an employer who already has a retirement plan, you must have it reviewed by a pension expert. According to the American Society of Pension Actuaries, the estimated cost to revise the existing 600,000 retirement plans in the United States may exceed $2.5 billion. The cost for a revision will depend on its complexity; small companies should anticipate up to a few thousand dollars to comply with the new law.

Plan amendments taking into account new contributions and benefit limits and other changes must be made in your plan year beginning after December 31, 1983. Technically, the plan will not lose its tax-qualified status before 1984 because it provides for benefits or contributions which exceed the new limitations. However, your deductible contributions for 1983 may not exceed the new limitations even though your plan has not yet been amended.

Simplified employee pension plans (SEPs)

A corporation or an unincorporated business may set up an administratively simple pension plan wherein the business makes deductible contributions to an IRA set up by each employee. Starting in plan years beginning after 1983, maximum contributions to SEPs are subject to the same limitation as profit-sharing and other defined-contribution plans: the lesser of $30,000 or 25% of compensation.

Top-heavy plans

To scale down benefits to owners and key employees, the new law imposes restrictions aimed to benefit rank-and-file employees. The restrictions apply to plans which are considered "top heavy." They must meet stricter vesting and minimum-benefit requirements in years beginning after 1983. These requirements apply to both corporate and self-employed plans.

Many small businesses and professional practices with plans that favor the owners will be considered top heavy and may be forced to disband if the cost of covering additional employees exceeds the benefits of the plan to the owners. One estimate predicts that 90% of existing defined-benefit plans are top heavy and will have to comply with the new requirements.

A top-heavy plan is one in which more than 60% of the contributions (in profit-sharing and other defined-contribution plans) or 60% of the accrued benefits (in a defined-benefit pension plan) are provided for key employees. Whether a plan is top heavy is an assessment that must be made each year. Key employees include officers, a more than 5% owner, a more than 1% owner with compensation over $150,000, and employees with the ten largest ownership interests. Further, any individual who was an officer or owner within the four preceding years is considered a key employee. Stock owned by family members will be attributed to employees under the constructive ownership rules.

If a single employer has more than one plan covering key employees, the top-heavy rules apply to the aggregated group. Plans of related employers must also be aggregated.

If a plan is top heavy it may consider only the first $200,000 of employee compensation in determining contributions or benefits. Starting in 1986, the $200,000 limit may be increased for post-1984 cost-of-living increases.

For years in which a plan is top heavy, one of two vesting schedules must be met: employees with three years of service have a nonforfeitable right to 100% of their accrued benefits from employer contributions, or employees' benefits are 100% vested after six years under a graded vesting schedule based on years of service.

Top-heavy plans will have to provide minimum contributions or benefits to employees who are not key employees. Generally, the minimum benefit under a defined-benefit plan is the lesser of 2% of average pay in the five highest consecutive earning years times years of service, or 20% of such average pay. For a defined-contribution plan, the minimum contribution for non-key employees would generally be 3% of compensation or, if lower, the contribution rate for the highest paid key employee would apply.

A 10% premature-withdrawal penalty will apply to distributions from top-heavy plans in years beginning after 1983 to key employees prior to age 59½. The penalty will not apply to distributions made because of the employee's disability or death. Further, a top-heavy plan will have to begin retirement distributions to key employees by the year in which they reach age 70½, even if they do not retire.

Corporate retirement plans

Corporate qualified retirement plans have traditionally provided maximum pension benefits for business owners and key executives. The corporation claims a tax deduction for its contributions; the employee need not report the contribution or earnings on the contribution as income. When benefits are paid, the employee includes them as income but may use special reporting methods to reduce the tax. These touchstones of pension law remain unchanged. However, the new tax law has lowered the amount of maximum contributions which corporations may make and ultimately the amount of benefits to be realized by highly paid executives.

The dollar limit for annual contributions to an employee account under a profit-sharing or other defined-contribution plan is reduced from $45,475 in 1982 to $30,000 after 1982. This $30,000 limit applies if it is less than the current percentage limitation, 25% of compensation.

Under a defined-benefit plan (a plan in which annual benefits upon retirement are fixed), the maximum amount of annual retirement benefits which a company can fund drops from $136,425 to $90,000. The $90,000 limit applies if it is less than the percentage limitation which has not been changed— 100% of average compensation for an employee's three highest consecutive earning years. However, top executives whose companies were funding a pension greater than $90,000 in 1982 will not have their benefits reduced because of the new $90,000 ceiling, provided that the firm had a qualifying defined benefit plan in existence on July 1, 1982. For plan years beginning after 1982, the firm may continue to fund the same pension as it did as of July 1, 1982 as long as the 1982 limit of $136,425 is not exceeded.

Existing pension and profit-sharing plans are subject to the new limits for plan years beginning after December 31, 1982. New plans not in existence on July 1, 1982, are immediately subject to the new limits.

Loans. In addition to saving for the future, retirement plans may be a source of current funds. Plans may permit loans to participants. Those in need of a down payment on a house or of college tuition have found loans from pension plans attractive because of reasonable interest rates and repayment terms. However, to discourage large loans, the new law applies these limitations: The maximum loan may not exceed $50,000 or one-half of an employee's vested retirement account, whichever amount is lower. Benefits are considered vested when rights to them are nonforfeitable. However, if a vested account is less than $20,000, up to $10,000 may be borrowed. Further, the payment term of a permissible loan may not exceed five years. However, the term of a loan made for the purpose of buying or rehabilitating a principal residence may exceed five years without tax. Loans outstanding on August 13, 1982, are generally not subject to these limitations unless the loan is renewed or renegotiated after that date.

A loan that does not meet the new tests may be taxed as a distribution of benefits.

70½ age test for company benefits. For plan years beginning after December 31, 1983, all qualified retirement plans must require that benefits begin in the year the employee reaches age 70½ unless retirement is delayed.

If an employee dies before his or her entire interest is paid, or payments are being made to a surviving spouse who dies before the entire interest is received, the balance will generally have to be distributed to the beneficiaries within five years. There is an exception if the employee had started to receive benefits over a period not exceeding the lives of the employee and his or her spouse.

Chapter 2
INVESTMENT PLANNING FOR RETIREMENT FUNDS

AMERICANS can no longer be complacent about retirement security for two good reasons. We are living longer, perhaps 20 years or more beyond age 65, and for many, Social Security is and will continue to be an inadequate basis of support. Therefore, advance planning is necessary to guarantee a secure retirement.

Fortunately, the tax laws are designed to encourage retirement savings. Tax-approved personal retirement plans offer two main advantages: You can accumulate large funds for retirement without tax erosion and enjoy the immediate benefit of deducting contributions. For example, if you set up an IRA at age 30 and contribute the maximum amount allowed each year until age 65, you will have accumulated more than half a million dollars if your money earns 10% compounded annually, $866,340 at 12%, or $1.7 million at 15%. Also, you will have saved a considerable amount of income taxes: $23,100 if you are in the 33% income tax bracket, $35,000 if you are in the top tax bracket. The following charts show how much can be accumulated, depending on your contributions and interest rates, as well as tax savings from deducting contributions.

The compounding of interest which accumulates tax free makes it possible for many Americans to become millionaires by undertaking a long-term retirement savings program. The earlier you start your savings program, the more you will have. You might ask, "What will a million dollars be worth 30 or 40 years from now?" No one can say with any certainty, but you may be sure that you will be better off with it than without it.

The major decisions in setting up a retirement account are how and where to invest your savings. Most investments, rang-

HOW TAX-FREE ANNUAL COMPOUNDING BUILDS UP YOUR RETIREMENT FUND

$2,000 invested annually at	Number of years invested							
	5	10	15	20	25	30	35	40
8%	$11,740	$28,980	$54,300	$91,520	$146,200	$226,580	$344,640	$518,020
10%	12,200	31,880	63,540	114,540	196,700	328,980	542,040	885,180
12%	12,700	35,100	74,560	144,100	266,660	482,660	866,340	1,534,160
15%	13,480	40,600	95,160	204,880	425,580	869,480	1,762,340	3,558,020

$4,000 invested annually at	Number of years invested							
	5	10	15	20	25	30	35	40
8%	$23,480	$57,960	$108,600	$183,040	$292,400	$453,120	$689,280	$1,036,040
10%	24,400	63,760	127,080	229,080	393,400	657,960	1,084,080	1,770,360
12%	25,400	70,200	149,120	288,200	533,320	965,320	1,732,680	3,068,320
15%	26,960	81,200	190,320	409,760	851,160	1,738,960	3,524,680	7,116,040

$10,000 invested annually at

				Number of years invested				
	5	10	15	20	25	30	35	40
8%	$58,700	$144,900	$271,500	$457,600	$731,000	$1,132,900	$1,723,200	$2,590,100
10%	61,000	159,400	317,700	572,700	983,500	1,664,900	2,710,200	4,425,900
12%	63,500	175,500	372,800	720,500	1,333,300	2,413,300	4,331,700	7,670,800
15%	67,400	203,000	475,800	1,024,400	2,127,900	4,347,400	8,811,700	17,790,100

$15,000 invested annually at

				Number of years invested				
	5	10	15	20	25	30	35	40
8%	$88,050	$217,350	$407,250	$686,400	$1,096,500	$1,699,350	$2,584,800	$3,885,150
10%	91,500	239,100	476,550	859,050	1,475,250	2,467,350	4,065,300	6,638,850
12%	95,250	263,250	550,200	1,080,750	1,999,950	3,619,950	6,497,550	11,506,200
15%	101,100	304,500	713,700	1,536,600	3,191,850	6,521,100	13,217,550	26,685,150

YOUR TAX SAVING FROM RETIREMENT PLAN CONTRIBUTIONS

Tax saving from annual $2,000 contribution

Tax bracket	5	10	15	20	25	30	35	40
19%	$1,900	$3,800	$5,700	$7,600	$9,500	$11,400	$13,300	$15,200
25%	2,500	5,000	7,500	10,000	12,500	15,000	17,500	20,000
33%	3,300	6,600	9,900	13,200	16,500	19,800	23,100	26,400
44%	4,400	8,800	13,200	17,600	22,000	26,400	30,800	35,200
50%	5,000	10,000	15,000	20,000	25,000	30,000	35,000	40,000

Tax saving from annual $4,000 contribution

Tax bracket	5	10	15	20	25	30	35	40
19%	$3,800	$7,600	$11,400	$15,200	$19,000	$22,800	$26,600	$30,400
25%	5,000	10,000	15,000	20,000	25,000	30,000	35,000	40,000
33%	6,600	13,200	19,800	26,400	33,000	39,600	46,200	52,800
44%	8,800	17,600	26,400	35,200	44,000	52,800	61,600	70,400
50%	10,000	20,000	30,000	40,000	50,000	60,000	70,000	80,000

Tax saving from annual $10,000 contribution

Tax bracket	5	10	15	20	25	30	35	40
19%	$9,500	$19,000	$28,500	$38,000	$47,500	$57,000	$66,500	$76,000
25%	12,500	25,000	37,500	50,000	62,500	75,000	87,500	100,000
33%	16,500	33,000	49,500	66,000	82,500	99,000	115,500	132,000
44%	22,000	44,000	66,000	88,000	110,000	132,000	154,000	176,000
50%	25,000	50,000	75,000	100,000	125,000	150,000	175,000	200,000

Tax saving from annual $15,000 contribution

Tax bracket	5	10	15	20	25	30	35	40
19%	$14,250	$28,500	$42,750	$57,000	$71,250	$85,500	$99,750	$114,000
25%	18,750	37,500	56,250	75,000	93,750	112,500	131,250	150,000
33%	24,750	49,500	74,250	99,000	123,750	148,500	173,250	198,000
44%	33,000	66,000	99,000	132,000	165,000	198,000	231,000	264,000
50%	37,500	75,000	112,500	150,000	187,500	225,000	262,500	300,000

ing from savings certificates to real estate, are open to you. However, yields, risks, and costs vary. Before you decide on an investment, consider the following facts:

1. How does an account fit into your retirement plans? Will it be the only source of funds, in addition to Social Security benefits, or do you have another pension plan? If you can count on other funds for retirement years, you may be willing to take greater risk with your investments. If the retirement account must provide most of your income during retirement, you should follow a more conservative path.

2. How many years do you have until retirement? If retirement is only a few years away, you may seek low-risk, income-oriented investments. Younger persons may be willing to accept higher risk or look for long-term growth.

3. How much risk can you comfortably tolerate? Your investment choice should not keep you awake at night. Only you can decide which investment suits your temperament. If you want to avoid risk as much as possible, invest in insured bank deposits or government securities.

Investing in savings certificates

Banks and savings and loan associations (S&Ls) have been aggressive competitors for retirement account dollars. It has been estimated that there is potentially more than $200 billion a year that could be saved in IRA plans alone. More conservative figures put potential IRA contributions at $10 to $50 billion annually.

Since IRAs were first introduced in 1977, banking institutions have attracted the overwhelming number of accounts; they held their lead even when the rules on IRAs were liberalized in 1981. According to a survey conducted for the American Bankers Association in mid-February 1982, over 70% of those who opened IRAs in the first six weeks of 1982 put their IRAs in commercial banks, S&Ls, and credit unions.

There are several good reasons for this popularity. Banks and S&Ls are conveniently located, familiar institutions. Bank officers are known to customers and can be questioned in person. Retirement accounts at savings institutions enjoy a high measure of safety. Accounts are insured by the FDIC or FSLIC for up to $100,000 in each bank; credit union accounts enjoy similar protection. There are usually no fees for opening or maintaining an account. Banking institutions may pay market rates, as well as enhance returns through interest compounding, and guarantee that return for a fixed term.

Today the banking industry is in the midst of deregulation. What this means to the retirement investor is an ever-increasing assortment of savings instruments from which to choose: fixed rate to variable rate; terms from a few days to eight years; daily, monthly, or annual compounding; minimum deposit requirements from zero to $20,000. Consider the present array of investment options found at savings institutions, the majority of which are certificates of deposit (CDs) with varying maturities and terms.

7- to 31-day maturity. The length of maturity is fixed by each institution. The minimum deposit is $20,000. Interest on the CDs is pegged to the three-month Treasury bill rate. S&Ls may pay ¼% more than commercial banks. Beginning May 1, 1983, the interest rate ceiling and the ¼% difference between commercial and savings banks will be eliminated; prior to that date, the rate and differential will be suspended whenever the 91-day T-bill rate is 9% or less for four consecutive months.

32- to 91-day maturity. This CD has a minimum deposit of $7500. Interest is tied to the 13-week Treasury bill discount rate and is not compounded. The bank may set the term of the CD at the outset of your investment.

Six-month certificate. This CD, also called the "money market certificate," is keyed to the rate on six-month Treasury bills. Interest is not compounded. The minimum deposit is $10,000.

18-month fixed rate. There is no interest-rate ceiling. Interest is set by the savings institution. Rates may vary considerably from bank to bank. There is no required minimum; each bank may set its own minimum.

18-month variable rate. The rate on these accounts is not guaranteed; they will vary with the rise and fall of similarly termed Treasury obligations. For those investors expecting a rise in interest rates, this CD offers the opportunity to obtain those high rates. As with the fixed-rate certificate, each bank may establish its own minimum deposit.

2½-year maturity. This CD, also called the "Small Saver" or 30-month CD, pays interest at rates keyed to similarly termed Treasury notes. Federal banking regulations do not set minimum investment requirements, although some banks have set their own minimum, such as $100, $250, or $500.

3½-year maturity. This CD also has no interest ceiling. Rates will approximate Treasury notes of similar maturity. For investors who believe rates have peaked, this CD offers the opportunity to lock in high yields. Minimum deposits are set by each institution.

Day-of-deposit accounts. These are regular savings accounts which figure interest from the day of deposit to the day of withdrawal. There are no minimum deposit requirements, but interest is low (currently 5.5% at S&Ls).

Federal credit unions no longer have federally imposed interest-rate ceilings, regardless of the type of account. Credit union investments account for almost 5% of this country's savings.

If you consider investing in a savings certificate, you should compare the offerings at several banks. Rates and methods of compounding interest vary. Also, some banks offer premiums, such as free checking, when you open a retirement account.

Which savings option is for you?

Your choice will be governed by several factors: how much you have to invest, how you expect interest rates to fluctuate, and your age.

Since you are investing IRA dollars, your choice is limited. No more than $2000 may be invested in any year; the certificates with minimum deposits of $7500, $10,000, and $20,000 are, of course, out of the question. It may be many years before you have sufficient IRA dollars which you can roll over into a higher yield CD. Each year you make an IRA contribution, it goes into a new CD; it will not be added to an existing one. A $2000 investment in a CD earning 12% would take almost 12 years before accumulating a sufficient amount to meet a $7500 minimum-deposit requirement. If you do not have $2000 in a lump sum but plan to contribute smaller amounts monthly, you may be forced into a low-yielding day-of-deposit account until you have the required minimum deposit for a higher yielding CD. Some banks may permit you to make additions to a CD as long as the initial deposit requirement is met. These additions would enjoy the same rate applied to the initial deposit. When you have larger sums to invest, such as from Keogh plan contributions or tax-free rollovers, more CD options become available.

In the past few years we have witnessed unprecedented volatility in interest rates. Given the fallibility of experts who have been unsuccessful in predicting the next rise or fall, you have to guess how interest rates will move before you choose the term of the CD. If you feel rates have peaked, it is to your advantage to choose a long-term CD to lock in the high rate. If you feel rates will rise, you should stay with short-term certificates; lacking minimum deposits for the 7- to 31-day or 32- to 91-day CDs, you may be forced to put your funds into a day-of-deposit account. Such a move is advisable only for the shortest possible time. Interest rates would have to rise considerably to offset the amount lost by keeping your money in a day-of-deposit account instead of a higher yielding CD.

Your age may influence your investment choice. Banks are free to waive premature withdrawal penalties for those age 59½ and over. If you are over 59½ and you know your bank has traditionally waived the penalty, perhaps you should choose the highest yielding CD, regardless of its term. If you find yourself in a long-term CD when rates rise, you can switch without penalty. Be aware, however, that banks do not have to waive the penalty, or even permit early withdrawals with penalties. One local New York bank successfully blocked a couple's premature withdrawal from a low-yielding CD; allowing premature withdrawal is within the bank's discretion.

Disadvantages of banking institutions

Despite the positive aspects of investing your retirement dollars in a banking institution, there are disadvantages.

The prime drawback is the lack of flexibility. You are generally locked into the term of the CD. If you must cash in your certificate before maturity, you may be subject to a substantial forfeiture of interest and principal, in addition to tax penalties. Also, if you choose a fixed-rate certificate, you benefit if interest rates dip but you lose out if rates rise.

Another disadvantage is that banking institutions can change their rules after you have opened an account. For instance, they may have traditionally waived premature withdrawal penalties for those age 59½ or over, but suddenly, and perhaps without announcement, they can reverse this practice.

Banking rules are changing frequently. Only a few years ago all banks in the neighborhood offered the same terms and interest rates. Now investment options vary from bank to bank. Not all banks offer the maximum rates permitted by law. Further, not all banks compound interest in the same manner. Whether interest is compounded daily or annually could mean a difference of about $25 on a $2000 2½-year CD paying 15%. Finally, each bank has its own policy on procedures concerning maturity of certificates. Some banks automatically renew the CD for another term at the current rate unless notified to the contrary; some banks will not renew a matured CD without express authority from you. If you fail to act, you may find your funds switched to a day-of-deposit account on maturity.

Investing in annuities offered by insurance companies

Insurance companies have long been in the business of selling annuities. Since the expansion of personal retirement plans, insurance companies have tailored their annuities to accept retirement plan contributions. An annuity is a contract that provides a guaranteed monthly income for life or for a term of years. For every $1000 invested, you will receive a certain amount each month after retiring. The amount you receive monthly depends on your life expectancy and on the return the company was able to earn on your investments.

The chief advantage of an annuity is the assurance that you can never outlive your capital. You are guaranteed a retirement income for your life or, if you choose, for the lives of you and your spouse. Further, you have complete freedom from investment management. The insurance company invests your contributions as it sees fit, although you may choose from certain types of investments, as discussed later.

Insurance company annuities offer another advantage in this age of mobility: continuity of investment if you move from your current location. Many insurance companies have offices nationwide and can continue to service your account. Even in the absence of a convenient office, you may take your contract with you anywhere and continue to pay premiums by mail.

Types of annuities and contract options. There are two general types of annuities: fixed rate and variable rate. With a fixed-rate annuity, you are guaranteed two rates: a maximum rate guaranteed only for the first year (in some cases two years) of the contract and a minimum rate guaranteed for the term of the contract. The maximum rate offered today approximates the return of a money market fund or one-year Treasury notes. In an insurance company brochure you may find a projection of earnings over the life of the contract based entirely on this high rate. Such a projection may be misleading since the high return is not guaranteed. The minimum return guaranteed by most companies today is low—4% to 6%.

The variable or flexible annuity offers no guaranteed rate. Your return varies with the type of investment. Generally, you may choose to have the insurance company invest in a stock fund, a money market fund, or a fixed-income fund with a guaranteed return which is adjusted periodically. There may be some opportunity to switch among the funds.

With either type of annuity you insure income until you die or until both you and your spouse die. The latter is called a "joint and survivor contract"; payments are actuarily reduced since they will be extended over the lives of both spouses.

An endowment policy may be used as a retirement plan. It provides for the payment of a definite sum after a stated number of years.

A feature unique to insurance company annuities is a disability rider. If you become disabled before your contract has been completed, the company will pay your premiums and continue your retirement account. Thus you receive the same retirement income as if you had not become disabled. Of course, you cannot claim a tax deduction for the insurance company's payment on behalf of your annuity.

Annuities tailored to retirement plans are required to contain certain features. An IRA annuity contract may not require premiums exceeding $2000. Any refund of premium or dividends must be applied toward the payment of the following year's premiums or toward the purchase of additional benefits. IRA annuity premiums must be "flexible," that is, the contract may not call for a fixed premium but must permit a fluctuating premium. The company may set a minimum annual premium, such as $500, below which they will not write a policy. The contract may not contain any loan provisions. Read the contract carefully. You have seven days from the day you receive the disclosure statement to change your mind without incurring a penalty.

Disadvantages of annuities

A major drawback of investing in annuities is their fees, which are generally classified as "front load" or "back load." In a "front load" annuity, there is an initial charge which is subtracted from every $1000 invested. One company charges almost $90 per $1000. Thus of a $2000 contribution, $180 will go directly to the insurance company and $1820 will be invested for your benefit. In addition to the initial fee, there may be a small annual maintenance fee.

In a "back load" annuity there is no initial fee, but annual maintenance charges beginning in the second year may be substantial—$25 or $30. The company may charge a penalty for early withdrawals from back-load annuities. The penalty, 7% or 8%, decreases each year so that there is no penalty after a certain year, such as the 8th, 10th, or 11th year. One company permits withdrawals of up to 10% of the fund before it imposes penalties. There may also be a small service charge for each withdrawal.

A second major disadvantage of insurance company annuities has been their poor investment return. High returns are not guaranteed beyond the first year or two. In the past, annuities have generally realized a low return compared to other investments.

Another drawback is the lack of legacy resulting from an annuity. If you die ten years or more after your annuity starts and did not select a joint and survivor annuity, your heirs receive nothing.

Finally, be aware that annuities are purchased through insurance agents who earn commissions on the sale of policies. Do not be pressured into a purchase which may not suit your needs.

Setting up an account with a broker

You may open a retirement account at a brokerage firm and choose either a self-directed account or a mutual fund operated by the firm. The main advantage of either type of account is flexibility. With a mutual fund you can share in a managed portfolio of investments, and within a mutual fund family you may switch among funds. In a self-directed account you choose how you wish to invest your money. Most investments, including stocks, bonds, real estate, and oil and gas, are open to you; you may switch or combine your holdings. Some brokerage firms also offer annuities similar to those offered by life insurance companies.

There is no one "right" investment for your retirement account. If you decide to open a self-directed account, you may design a plan to meet your needs and follow investments you think will succeed. Overseeing a personalized plan may be enjoyable, but it requires more effort than other options.

To fund your account, you should consider investments in light of your objectives, preferences, and tolerance for risk. You should also consider the past and present performance of various investments. A study by Roger G. Ibbotson of the University of Chicago's Graduate of School of Business and by Rex A.

Sinquefield of the American National Bank & Trust Company of Chicago compared selected investments from 1926 through 1978. Common stocks (as indicated by Standard & Poor's 500 Stock Index) led the group with an average annual return of 9%, more than twice the annual return of corporate bonds and Treasury obligations during that period. Inflation in those years averaged 2.5% annually. However, stocks are generally adversely affected by periods of high inflation and have not fared as well recently.

Looking at a shorter period, in a survey by Salomon Brothers, Inc., bonds were the only major investment that had a return higher than inflation for the year ending June 1, 1982. That news may come as a surprise considering the long slump in the bond market. But the survey also showed that the bond market's performance in previous years was no match for last year's yield of 11.4%. In the measure of average annual returns for the past ten years, bonds placed last with a return of 3.6%. Stocks were only slightly higher, with a 3.9% return. Of course, you should consider the performance of stocks of individual companies and current economic conditions.

New investment instruments are being designed to take advantage of the retirement account market. For example, zero-coupon bonds are corporate bonds that may be suited to retirement accounts. They are sold at a deep discount from face value and pay no periodic interest. The yield is the difference between the price paid and the face value received at redemption.

An advantage of zero-coupon bonds is that your return is known in advance. And there is little chance that the bonds will be called. However, if you buy zero-coupon bonds, be prepared to hold them since the market is currently limited and commissions reduce your gain.

Zero-coupon bonds, like other corporate bonds, are not insured. Seek reliable companies since you do not receive any income for several years until the bond matures. Some brokers now sell zero-coupon bank certificates of deposit which are federally insured to $100,000.

Another investment variation designed for retirement accounts is limited partnerships which emphasize income instead of tax deductions. For example, Merrill Lynch offers a royalty partnership which invests in oil and gas and an income realty fund which purchases income-producing real estate. The minimum deposit for each of these accounts is $1000. You pay a broker's commission plus the fee for setting up a retirement account.

Some limited partnerships are speculative and designed for those willing to gamble a part of their retirement savings. Consider only investments offered through established firms and organized by companies with experience in the field. If you are not familiar with the operations of a partnership, have your financial advisor examine the prospectus.

Disadvantages of an account with a broker

Cost is the major disadvantage of establishing an account with a broker. If you invest in a brokerage mutual fund program, you can expect to pay a setup cost of $15 to $20 and an annual fee of about $20. If you switch among funds, you pay a fee of about $5 for each transaction. A self-directed account is more expensive, with setup fees running $25 to $30 and annual maintenance fees of $35 to $50. Some firms charge a flat annual fee of about $50. Others may charge a fee equal to a percentage of your portfolio, such as $\frac{2}{10}$ of 1%, on top of a minimum annal fee. In addition to these fees, you pay the broker's commission for buying and selling securities. Some brokers charge more if the account holds a particular kind of investment; some may charge termination fees if you decide to move your account.

Note that investing in securities is more practical when you have saved a few thousand dollars. Some investment advisors suggest that self-directed plans be postponed for the first few years until a fund can be built up. Otherwise, if you plan to buy stocks you will be forced to buy in odd lots or buy lower priced stock, and much of your investment will be eaten up by commissions.

When you invest with a brokerage firm, there is no certainty of investment return or yield. Rates and earnings are not fixed.

Check to see if an account is protected by the Securities Investors Protection Corporation (SIPC). Coverage extends to $500,000 for securities and to $100,000 for cash held in a protected account. SIPC insurance guards only against insolvency of the firm or mismanagement of your account. There is no guarantee against ordinary market losses.

Investing in mutual funds

Mutual funds have traditionally offered the small investor a way to invest in the market with low minimum requirements. By pooling the money of many individuals, funds enable each investor to share in a large, diversified portfolio and spread the market risks. Mutual funds have grown in popularity; they held $241.4 billion in assets at the end of 1981. Part of their growth is due to the rapid rise in deposits in money market funds, especially in the late 1970s when interest rates soared.

In addition to small minimums and good returns, mutual funds offer professional management and a high degree of liquidity. While the funds' professional management is not a guarantee of success, it means that the individual investor does not have to study the market. The liquidity offered by the funds assures easy deposits and withdrawals and no penalties. In fact, money market funds are often used by institutional investors and individuals as a temporary parking place for cash that will later be invested in another instrument.

There are two types of mutual funds: open end and closed end. In an open-end fund, investment companies offer shares to the public continuously. The price of a share is determined by the value of a fund's portfolio, plus other assets and minus liabilities. This figure, divided by the number of shares owned by shareholders, is the fund's net asset value per share, or price. Note that money market funds are an exception; their price usually remains constant at $1 per share. An open-end company will repurchase shares on demand at the prevailing value per share.

A closed-end fund issues a limited number of shares which are traded on stock exchanges. These funds are not obligated to repurchase shares. Prices or net asset values per share (abbreviated NAV) for open-end and closed-end funds can be found in the financial pages of major newspapers. The following discussion is limited to the more common open-end mutual funds.

Before the tax law changes became effective in 1982, mutual funds accounted for 27.3% of the Keogh market and 9.6% of the IRA market. A mutual fund offers flexibility at low cost.

Funds that are "no loads" do not carry any sales charges. Setup fees and transfer fees may be small or nonexistent, and annual maintenance fees may total only $5 or $10. You may incur a small charge if you terminate an account. "Load" funds are sold through brokers or salespersons, and you pay a commission of 6% to 8½%. Fees are paid separately and do not reduce your investment.

A fund may purchase stocks, corporate bonds, money market instruments, government securities, and international investments; it may emphasize growth or income, or aim for both. A fund family is a group of funds managed by the same company. The advantage of a family is that you can easily move your money among the different funds as economic conditions change.

Types of funds

Money market funds—also called liquid asset or cash funds, invest in high-yield money market instruments such as U.S. government securities, bank certificates of deposit, and commercial paper.

Stock funds—invest mainly in equities; they may purchase common and/or preferred stock. Some may concentrate on a particular industry or on companies in a particular area.

Corporate bond funds—invest mainly in company bonds. These funds usually emphasize income rather than growth.

Municipal bond funds—invest in tax-exempt bonds of cities, states, and other local governments.

Aggressive growth funds—emphasize growth or capital appreciation and accept greater risk to achieve it. For example, an aggressive growth fund may borrow money to leverage its investments or use options.

Growth funds—seek long-term capital growth. These funds usually invest in common stocks that have growth potential.

Income funds—try to provide immediate income from dividends and interest instead of long-term growth.

Growth and income funds—aim for both capital appreciation and current income.

Balanced funds—invest in a balance of common stocks and fixed-income instruments, such as preferred stocks and corporate bonds. With their conservative investment policy, the value of these funds generally does not fluctuate as widely as the market.

Option income funds—invest in dividend-paying common stocks on which call options are traded on the major exchanges. These funds accept the risks involved in options to provide high income.

Disadvantages of investing in a mutual fund

Using mutual funds for your retirement account has drawbacks, primarily a lack of assured return and the absence of insurance. The return fluctuates with market conditions. In the past few years money market funds have had high annual returns, but there is no assurance that such yields will continue. The best way to assess the reliability of a particular fund is to check its record over the past several years. Three investment services that publish this information are: United Business Service, Weisenberger Investment Companies Source, and Tipper Analytical Services.

Which fund is for you?

If you do opt for mutual funds, the experts recommend that you diversify into different types of funds within a mutual fund family. For example, you could use both a money market fund and a stock fund.

Some tax authorities advise against stock funds for retirement accounts for two reasons: losses are not deductible; and earnings, part of which would be capital gains, would normally be taxed at a maximum of 20%, but in a retirement fund all earnings are considered ordinary income at withdrawal and subject to tax of up to 50%. Other authorities, however, suggest that stock funds emphasizing growth may be ideal for younger workers who can wait out the short-term losses and look to long-term gains.

Also not recommended by most investment advisors for retirement accounts are tax-exempt funds, which usually pay a slightly lower return, because their tax-free feature is wasted.

All retirement account withdrawals are taxed as ordinary income.

Government bonds

United States Individual Retirement Bonds, designed for IRAs, are no longer sold, though outstanding Retirement Bonds continue to earn interest at 9%, compounded semiannually to 9.2%. Interest is paid only upon redemption; the rate is guaranteed until age 70½ when interest stops accruing and the bonds must be redeemed.

Diversifying your investments

You may set up a retirement plan and select one investment vehicle in that year and choose another the next year. You may also split your contribution between two or more investments. For example, you are eligible to contribute $2000 to an IRA. You may choose to put $500 into a stock fund, $1000 into an individual retirement account at your local bank, and $500 into a money market fund. But consider whether you will get the best return on your investment if you put less than $2000 into a particular instrument. For example, some banks may limit the top interest rate to IRA accounts with the maximum contribution of $2000. If you deposit only $1000 in an IRA account, you may receive a lower interest rate.

Institution	Investments	Return
Banks, thrifts, credit unions	Savings certificates	Tied to Treasury rates
	Passbook saving account	5¼% at commercial banks, 5½% at thrift higher at credit unions
Insurance companies	Fixed-premium front-load annuities	Fixed for one year at a time
	Back-load flexible premium annuities	Fluctuates
Brokerage	Self-directed: stocks, bonds, unit investment trusts, government obligations, limited partnerships	Fluctuates
	Load funds: funds investing in stocks, bonds, money market instruments, options, commodities	Fluctuates
Mutual fund families	No-load funds: funds investing in stocks, bonds, money market instruments, options, commodities	Fluctuates
	Load funds: funds investing in stocks, bonds, money market instruments, options, commodities	Fluctuates

ety	Opening fees	Annual management fees	Withdrawal penalties
ranteed by DIC/FSLIC	None	Generally none	Six months' interest on maturities of one year or more; no penalties at credit unions
ranteed by DIC/FSLIC	None	None	None
	8%–9%	About $8–$10	None
	0–$30	About $25–$30	7%–8%; declines 1% each year and ends after first 7 to 10 years
guarantee against arket losses, your ccount is guaranteed y SIPC against mis-anagement or in-olvency of the firm	0–$30	$25–$50, plus commissions. Possibly a fee equal to a percentage of your portfolio	None
ranteed by PC	$15–$20	About $20, plus $5 to switch among funds	None
	0–$5	$10 or less; free switching	None
	6%–8½%	$10 or less; $5 to switch among funds	None

Chapter 3
YOUR IRA

THE tax shelter advantages of IRAs are designed to encourage every person who has earned income to save for retirement. You have earned income if you have wage or salary income or are self-employed as a business owner or professional.

Setting up an IRA is simple. You do not need special IRS approval for your plan as is generally necessary for Keogh and corporate retirement plans. Banks, brokerage firms, and insurance companies offering IRA investment plans will provide you with all necessary forms.

You may set up your IRA plan as an individual retirement acccount or an individual retirement annuity.

What is an individual retirement account?

Technically, an individual retirement account is a trust or custodial account. The trustee or custodian can be either the savings institution, brokerage firm, or mutual fund with which you have opened your IRA account. The trustee or custodian invests your funds according to the plan you have selected. Thus if you have invested in a certificate of deposit (CD) at your local bank, the bank acts as custodian for your CD. Generally, no fee is charged by a savings institution for an individual retirement account. The cost of other accounts is discussed in Chapter 2.

If you want a more active investment role, you may set up a "self-directed" plan. You make your own investment decisions while a bank, brokerage firm, or other institution or trustee handles your account. The fees for a self-directed plan may be high, so it may not pay to set up such an account until you have built up a sizable IRA fund.

You set up your self-directed plan following a Treasury model form. The model trust (Form 5305) and the model custodian account agreement (Form 5305A) meet the requirements of an exempt IRA. You do not need a ruling or determination letter approving the exemption of the account as is required of other qualified retirement plans. If you have a self-directed IRA, you may not invest in collectibles, such as coins, stamps, antique rugs, or artwork. Assets used to acquire collectibles are treated as distributions and are taxed to you.

What is an individual retirement annuity?

An individual retirement annuity is an annuity contract or an endowment contract issued by an insurance company which pays a specified amount monthly beginning at age 59½, or at retirement, and continuing for life. The annuity contract may be on your life or may be a joint and survivor contract for the benefit of you and your spouse. No trustee or custodian is required. The contract, endorsed to meet the terms of an IRA, is all that is required.

In the case of an endowment contract, no deduction is permitted for the portion of the premium allocable to life insurance. This nondeductible amount is referred to as P.S. 85 and will be supplied by your insurance agent.

The contract will not contain loan provisions because borrowing or pledging of the contract is not allowed under an IRA.

The contract must not have fixed premiums or annual premiums exceeding $2000.

Insurance company fees for an IRA annuity may be steep, especially in the early years of the contract. Determine how much of your annual contribution is actually for the purchase of an annuity and how much covers insurance company charges.

IRA break-even point for younger workers

Younger workers, especially those facing large financial obligations, such as purchase of a home or business, or college education for their children, may be reluctant to tie up their funds in an IRA. There is good reason for hesitating. The tax law imposes a tax penalty for withdrawals before age 59½, except in the case of disability. The fund is virtually frozen until that time. However, the money is yours, and if you need it you may pay the penalty and still come out ahead, depending on your tax bracket, investment return, and how long you have been contributing. The following chart shows in which year you can withdraw your IRA funds and not lose any money.

BREAK-EVEN YEAR FOR PREMATURE WITHDRAWALS

	For investment yielding:			
Your tax bracket	8%	10%	12%	15%
19%	16	13	11	9
25%	13	11	9	7
33%	11	9	8	6
44%	10	8	7	6
50%	10	8	7	6

Contributing to a company plan

Your company may provide an opportunity for you to make voluntary IRA contributions to the company plan. The advantages of making voluntary contributions is that the funds are invested by the trustees of the plan. Starting with company plan years beginning after 1983, you will have to start distributions from employer-sponsored plans by age 70½ unless you continue working.

The rules for employer-sponsored IRA plans are generally the same as for personal IRAs. Distributions do not qualify for ten-year averaging. Penalties similar to those imposed under the IRA provisions are imposed on early withdrawal of deductible contributions from a qualified plan. Rollovers from an employer plan may be made to an IRA without incurring any withdrawal penalty, subject to the rule which limits rollovers to one per year.

Voluntary contributions to a company plan may not be made for your spouse. If you want to cover your spouse, you must set up an IRA outside of the company plan.

You do not have to count voluntary contributions to a company plan as your personal IRA deductible contribution. Voluntary contributions can accumulate tax free in the company fund while at the same time you can make a separate tax-deductible contribution to a personal IRA if you have additional available funds. If you follow this practice, you must specifically designate the voluntary contributions as nondeductible. Failure to make a designation automatically results in the treatment of voluntary contributions as deductible IRA contributions, thereby limiting the amount of IRA contributions you may make outside the plan. For example, your employer's plan allows you to make an annual voluntary contribution of $750. In 1982 you contribute $750 but do not designate the payment as nondeductible. You may then contribute only up to $1250 ($2000 − $750) to an IRA set up outside of the company plan for a total deduction of $2000. If you designate the $750 as nondeductible, you may contribute and deduct up to $2000 to your personal IRA.

Even though voluntary contributions are deductible, your employer is required to withhold FICA taxes on payroll deductions that go into the plan.

Check with your employer's plan administrator to determine when voluntary contributions must be made to avoid losing a contribution deduction. While you have until April 15, 1983, to make an IRA contribution for 1982, your employer is allowed, but not required, to treat contributions made in 1983 as 1983 contributions.

Figuring your contribution

Each year you may contribute and deduct 100% of your compensation up to $2000 to an IRA. Thus if you work part time and earn $2000, you may make the maximum IRA contribution. If both you and your spouse work, your total allowed deduction is $4000. You may deduct the contribution whether or not you itemize deductions.

You do not have to contribute the maximum even though you are qualified to do so. You may contribute any amount you want up to the maximum. You may change your contribution each year, for example, contributing the maximum one year and a lesser amount the next. Be aware, however, that some high-yield investments are open only to those contributing $2000. If you contribute less than the maximum one year, you may not make it up in a later year.

Different contribution limits apply to IRAs for nonworking spouses and IRAs for divorcees, discussed later in this chapter.

Your deductible contribution must be based on payments received for rendering personal services, such as salary, wages, commissions, tips, fees, bonuses, or self-employed earned income. Net losses from self-employment do not reduce wages earned as an employee. Thus if you are employed and have a sideline business that suffers a loss, you may base an IRA contribution on your wages, regardless of the size of the loss. However, if your only income is from your unincorporated business which suffers a loss, you may not claim an IRA deduction.

Compensation does not include investment income, such as interest, dividends, or profits from sales of property. A trader whose sole income was derived from stock dividends and gains in buying and selling stocks set up an IRA and deducted his contribution. The IRS disallowed the deduction on the grounds that his income was not earned income. The trader argued that compensation is a broad term which should include his profits from investments. His trading activities were more than those of a mere investor. He had his own desk at a national brokerage house, worked full time at his investment activities, and traded over $3 million during the year. He did not file a Schedule C or pay self-employment tax. Despite his substantial investment activities, the Tax Court sided with the IRS. His profits came from property holdings and are not considered earned income.

The IRS stated in private letter rulings that compensation does not include disability payments or retirement pay.

You may not base an IRA contribution on income earned abroad for which the foreign earned income exclusion is claimed.

The compensation must actually be earned by you. If you live in a community-property state, the fact that one-half of your spouse's income is considered yours does not entitle you to make contributions to an IRA based on that income.

As long as you have earnings, you may contribute to an IRA even though you are receiving a pension or Social Security benefits.

Age limit on contributions

There is no minimum age requirement for contributions to an IRA. Children with earnings are permitted to make contributions.

You may not deduct contributions made in the year you reach age 70½. Thus individuals born in June 1912 or earlier may not make IRA contributions for 1982. However, if your employer makes a contribution to your account under an SEP, you may claim a deduction (see Chapter 6).

Further, once you reach age 70½, you must begin to take distributions from your IRA. If you make voluntary payments to your employer's qualified plan, you may not claim a deduction in the year you reach age 70½. Also, you must start taking distributions if you reach age 70½ during a company plan year beginning after 1983 unless you continue working.

When to make contributions

You may make your contribution until the due date for filing your returns, plus any extensions. Thus a contribution for 1982 may be made any time during 1982 but no later than April 15, 1983 (plus extensions). You may not make a contribution before the start of the calendar year; your 1983 contribution may not be made before January 1, 1983.

You do not have to make your entire contribution at once. You may contribute a small amount each month or several larger installments until you reach your maximum. Some banks will arrange with your employer to have your contributions made via payroll deductions. However, check whether your investment vehicle will accept periodic contributions. For example, if your IRA is in 18-month bank certificates and you contribute $1000 in January when the rate is 14%, you will not automatically get the same rate on a $1000 contribution in July. Your July contribution will earn interest at the then-prevailing rate.

Your available cash will influence the timing of your contributions. If you have the cash to make a contribution at any time, consider doing so as early in the year as possible because earnings will accumulate tax free. One bank has claimed that making contributions at the beginning rather than at the end of each year means that approximately $50,000 more will accumulated after 30 years of contributions.

IRAs for married couples

If both you and your spouse have earned income, each of you may set up an IRA account up to $2000.

EXAMPLES—

1. You earn a salary of $20,000; your spouse earns $10,000. Both of you are eligible to set up the IRA plans. On a joint return the maximum deduction is $4000. If only one of you works and qualifies to set up an IRA, the maximum deduction is $2000, unless an account for a nonworking spouse is set up.
2. You live in a community-property state. You earn a salary of $20,000. Your spouse does not work. The maximum deduction for an IRA is $2000, even though under the community-property laws your spouse is considered to have earned half your salary. You may set up an IRA for your nonworking spouse. In that case, your maximum deduction may not exceed $2250.

Account for nonworking spouse. If you are eligible to contribute to an IRA, you may also make deductible contributions on behalf of your nonworking spouse. You may have two separate IRAs, one for you and one for your spouse, or a single IRA which has a subaccount for you and another subaccount for your spouse. A joint account is not allowed. However, each spouse may have a right of survivorship in the subaccount of the other.

If you already have an IRA for yourself and you want to make contributions on behalf of your nonworking spouse, you may do so by opening a new IRA for your spouse and continuing your present IRA for yourself. However, if you have an annuity or endowment contract, check with your insurance agent about any contract restrictions on reducing your premium payments. Before setting up a single IRA with subaccounts for you and your spouse, check Treasury regulations covering their use.

If you set up an account (or a subaccount) for your spouse, your spouse must not have any compensation, including tax-exempt foreign earned income for the year. Suppose your spouse stopped working on December 31, 1981, and received a final paycheck on January 5, 1982. According to the IRS, under the spousal account rules you may not make a contribution in 1982 to your spouse's account even if your spouse is not employed at any time during 1982 because your spouse received pay during 1982. On the other hand your spouse may receive any amount of unearned income, such as interest, dividends, or Social Security benefits, and contributions on your spouse's behalf are deductible.

No deduction for a spousal IRA may be claimed for the year in which either spouse reaches age 70½ or for any year thereafter. However, if the working spouse is under 70½, that spouse may continue making contributions on his or her own behalf under the regular IRA rules. Congress is considering a bill that would allow a working spouse over age 70½ to continue making contributions to the account of the younger, non-working spouse. Under the proposal, the contribution would be limited to $2000 and would be allocated to the account of the nonworking spouse.

If you are divorced, you may not maintain a spousal account for your former spouse. If you contributed to an account on behalf of your nonworking spouse and divorce later in the year, the contribution is an excess contribution. IRAs based on alimony are discussed later in this chapter.

An amount distributed to one spouse may not be rolled over to an IRA account of the other spouse, except in the case of divorce.

IRAs for divorcées

A divorced spouse with little or no earnings is allowed a limited deduction for contributions to an IRA established by the former spouse at least five years before the divorce, provided the former spouse contributed to the account in at least three of the five years preceding the divorce. The divorced spouse's deduction is limited to the lesser of $1125 or compensation plus alimony received. A divorced spouse with earnings above this amount need not rely on these special rules but may make IRA contributions of 100% of earnings up to $2000.

EXAMPLES—

1. A divorced spouse whose former spouse contributed to an IRA for the past five years receives $6000 in alimony but does not work. Her IRA contribution is limited to $1125.

2. Same facts as above except the divorced spouse earns $3000 from a part-time job. An IRA contribution of up to $2000 may be made.

How distributions are taxed

All distributions from an IRA, whether paid in a lump sum or as an annuity, are taxed as ordinary income. Distributions do not qualify for special ten-year averaging. However, the regular five-year averaging method may be used to reduce the current tax.

Special retirement bonds. In the past, one IRA investment alternative was the purchase of special U.S. Retirement Bonds, which the Treasury stopped issuing on April 30, 1982. If you redeemed a bond in 1982 which was held for 12 months or less and for which you claimed a deduction in 1981, the proceeds are taxable in 1982. If you redeemed a bond in 1982 which was purchased earlier in the year and for which no deduction is claimed, the proceeds are not taxable. Bonds held 12 months or less earn no interest. If bonds are held more than 12 months, proceeds are taxable in the year the bonds are redeemed. However, you must report the full proceeds in the year you reach age 70½ even if you do not redeem the bonds.

Activities that trigger distribution treatment. Certain investments or activities are forbidden to an IRA. If you engage in one, you are treated as if you received a distribution even though no funds were actually distributed to you.

An investment in collectibles by a self-directed IRA is treated as a distribution. Collectibles include art, rugs, antiques, gems, stamps, coins, and similar items.

If you use your IRA or part of it as security for a loan, the pledged portion is treated as a distribution. If you borrow from your IRA annuity, you are considered to have received the entire amount in your contract. Further, your IRA loses its tax-exempt status.

If you are charged with any of these distributions and you are not yet age 59½, you will be liable for a penalty for premature distributions, discussed later in this chapter.

Withholding. Starting in 1983, tax will be withheld on IRA distributions, unless you make a special election to avoid withholding on the payments.

The party making the distribution must notify you of your right to avoid withholding. The Treasury has provided these notification guidelines: The payor must give notice of withholding options no later than the date of the first payment after 1982. The notice will instruct you that if the election is not made, income tax will be withheld as if you were married with three exemptions. No withholding is taken from non-deductible contributions you have made and on annual distributions of less than $5,400.

If you elect to avoid withholding, be sure that you do not run afoul of the estimated tax rules; otherwise you may be liable for a penalty.

Reporting requirements for IRAs

To date you do not have to file any special forms with the IRS to report the opening of your IRA, contributions to your plans, or earnings on your contributions. You merely claim your contribution deduction on your tax return. However, the IRS is considering new reporting rules for returns in 1983 and later years.

By June 30 of each year, your IRA custodian or trustee is required to furnish you with a statement of earnings on your account. Some banks or other custodians or trustees give reports more frequently.

Reporting is required if you make a tax-free rollover. The

rollover is reported on your tax return for information purposes. To date, no special form has been required; a line on Form 1040 may be used.

Reporting is also required if you are liable for a penalty for premature withdrawals, excess contributions, or insufficient withdrawals. You file Form 5329 with your return if you are liable for any of these penalties. Failure to file Form 5329 may result in an additional penalty of $10 per day (up to a maximum of $5000).

Bank penalties on closing time-deposit accounts before maturity

If you invest your IRA funds in a time-deposit account or savings certificate at a bank, you may have to pay a penalty if you close the account before maturity. If the term of the account is one year or less, the penalty is three months' interest. If it is more than one year, the penalty is six months' interest.

The penalty may be waived in certain circumstances. There is no penalty on the transfer of funds from an IRA in existence in December 1981 to an 18-month flexible rate IRA within the same institution. Banks are also permitted to waive the penalty for those age 59½ and over; most banks have chosen to do so. There is no penalty at credit unions.

Depending on how long the account has been open, a penalty may result in the forfeiture of some principal.

EXAMPLE—

You invest your $2000 IRA contribution in a 2½-year savings certificate earning 12% compounded monthly. You wish to withdraw your money after two months. Your account has earned $40 in interest. Your penalty is six months' interest, or $143. The balance of the penalty, $103 ($143 − $40), will be deducted from principal.

When interest rates rise and your money is tied up in a low-interest account, ask the bank to determine whether it pays you to incur the penalty by closing out the account and transferring your funds to an account paying higher interest.

EXAMPLE—

You invested $2000 in a 10% four-year account of which there remains a term of 2½ years. You have the option of switching to a 14% 2½-year account. Interest in both accounts is compounded annually. If you held the 10% account to maturity, you would have $2928. However, if you switch to the 14% account, you would have $3073 even after paying a penalty of $100.

Avoiding excess contribution penalties

Contributions over allowable amounts are penalized. If you contribute more than the amount allowed as a deduction, the excess contribution may be subject to a penalty tax of 6%. The penalty tax is cumulative. That is, unless you correct the excess, you will be subject to another penalty in the following year on the excess contribution. The penalty tax is not deductible.

EXAMPLE—

You contribute $2000 to an IRA earning 10%, but you were only entitled to contribute $1500 because you earned only $1500 from part-time work. Your penalty is $30 (6% of the $500 excess contribution) unless you correct the contribution.

The penalty tax on excess contributions may be avoided as follows: (1) An excess contribution, if not larger than $2250 ($15,000 in the case of SEP contributions) and if a deduction for the excess was not allowed, may be withdrawn at any time and the distribution treated as if it were never contributed (contributions in excess of $2250, or $15,000 in the case of SEP contributions, must be withdrawn prior to the due date for filing your return in order to avoid a penalty). (2) If an excess rollover contribution was made because of reliance on erroneous information, the $2250 limitation is increased to the extent of the excess contribution attributable to the erroneous information. (3) Excess contributions which are not withdrawn may be deducted in later years in which there is an unused deduction limitation.

EXAMPLE—

In 1981 you contributed $1500, but you were entitled to con-
tribute only $1200. If you are entitled to deduct $2000 in 1982,
you may correct your excess 1981 contribution by undercon-
tributing $300. Your deduction for 1981 is $1200. Your deduction for 1982 is $2000 (the $1700 you actually contributed
in 1982 plus the carryover of the excess contribution from
1981).

Premature distributions may be subject to penalty

The law imposes a penalty if you withdraw IRA funds before
age 59½ and are not disabled. You will be subject to a penalty
tax of 10% on the premature distribution even if the money is
needed for an emergency. The 10% tax is in addition to the tax
that will be incurred when you include the distribution as ordinary income with your other income.

EXAMPLE—

An unmarried man, age 40, withdraws $3000 from his IRA
plan. Assume that after including the $3000 distribution in in-
come, he is in the 35% tax bracket. Tax on the distribution is
$1050 (35% of $3000). To this amount he must add 10% of
$3000, or $300. His total tax on the distribution is $1350,
leaving him a net distribution of $1650 ($3000 − $1350).

Redemption of U.S. Retirement Bonds before age 59½ is
considered a premature distribution.

The penalty is figured only with reference to age and has
nothing to do with actual retirement. Thus if you retire at age
58 and take a distribution, you are subject to a penalty.

If you borrow on your annuity contract, you are considered
to have received your entire interest. Borrowing will subject
the fair market value of the contract to tax at ordinary income
rates as of the first day of the taxable year of the borrowing.
Your IRA loses its tax-exempt status. As a practical matter,
you are prohibited from borrowing since your contract may not
contain a loan provision.

If you use the account or part of it as security for a loan, the pledged portion is treated as a distribution. The payment of an overdue premium in the form of a loan against the cash surrender value of the contract is considered a distribution. A taxable rollover contribution, such as a second rollover within a 12-month period, is subject to a penalty if you are not age 59½. See Chapter 9 for further details.

You will not be liable for a premature distribution if you are correcting an excess contribution that did not exceed $2250.

How much must you withdraw at age 70½?

The law requires that you start receiving certain distributions from your account no later than the end of the year you reach age 70½. If you do not start receiving distributions from your plan by age 70½ or if you receive an insufficient distribution after this age, a penalty tax of 50% applies to the difference between the amount you should have received and the amount you did receive.

EXAMPLE—

You receive $500 from your IRA plan. The minimum amount required to be paid to you was $700. You pay a penalty tax of $100 (50% of $200).

The required installment amount is generally fixed by the amount of the account at age 70½ and your life expectancy. The IRS provides life expectancy figures. If you are married, you may figure the minimum distribution on the basis of the life expectancies of you and your spouse. This will result in a smaller minimum distribution requirement than for single individuals.

If you are age 70½, working, and have an SEP-IRA, you must still begin to receive distributions even though your employer is making contributions to your account.

If you have a spousal IRA and you are age 70½ but your spouse is younger, your spouse does not have to receive distributions.

The following table shows when payments must begin for those born in the following years:

PAYOUT TIMETABLE

Born in:	Begin distributions by December 31 of:
July 1911 through June 1912	1982
July 1912 through June 1913	1983
July 1913 through June 1914	1984
July 1914 through June 1915	1985
July 1915 through June 1916	1986

Figuring minimum payouts beginning at age 70½. Take the value of the account as of January 1 and divide it by 15 if you are an unmarried woman or by 12.1 if you are an unmarried man. The calculation will change in the following years as explained below.

EXAMPLE—

You are 70½ and your IRA account is valued at $60,000 on January 1, 1982. If you are a woman, you must withdraw $4000 ($60,000 ÷ 15) or more to avoid penalty in 1982; if you are a man, you must withdraw $4959 ($60,000 ÷ 12.1).

If you are married, you divide the value of the account by one of these multiples, depending on the age of your spouse.

MINIMUM PAYOUT MULTIPLES

	Age of spouse (in year you became age 70½)												
	61	62	63	64	65	66	67	68	69	70	71	72	73
Wife (owner)	21.6	21.1	20.7	20.3	19.9	19.6	19.2	18.9	18.6	18.3	18.0	17.8	17.5
Husband (owner)	23.0	22.4	21.8	21.2	20.7	20.2	19.7	19.2	18.7	18.3	17.9	17.5	17.1

	Age of spouse (in year you became age 70½)											
	74	75	76	77	78	79	80	81	82	83	84	85
Wife (owner)	17.3	17.1	16.9	16.7	16.6	16.4	16.3	16.2	16.0	15.9	15.8	15.8
Husband (owner)	16.7	16.4	16.1	15.8	15.5	15.2	14.9	14.7	14.5	14.3	14.1	13.9

EXAMPLE—

In June 1982 you become 70½. Your account has accumulated $40,000 as of January 1, 1982. Your wife is age 70 in 1982. You must withdraw $2186 ($40,000 ÷ 18.3) or more in 1982 to avoid a penalty tax for insufficient withdrawals.

The minimum distribution is refigured each year to produce an increasingly larger distribution until the entire fund is exhausted. This is accomplished by reducing the dividing number by one each year. For example, in the year you reach age 71½ the dividing number for an unmarried woman is 14 (15 − 1); for an unmarried man, the dividing number is 11.1 (12.1 − 1).

The IRS may waive the penalty for insufficient withdrawals if due to reasonable error and if steps are being taken to remedy the situation. You must submit evidence to account for shortfalls in withdrawals and show you are rectifying the situation. The IRS has indicated that examples of acceptable reasons for insufficient withdrawals include erroneous advice from the sponsoring organization or other pension advisors or that your own good-faith efforts to apply the required withdrawal formula produced a miscalculation. Attach your letter of explanation to Form 5329. You must pay the penalty tax; if the IRS grants you a waiver, it will refund the penalty.

Recordkeeping for your IRA

Over the course of your working career you may contribute tens of thousands of dollars to your IRA. However, in all likelihood all your money will not be in one place. Further, you may move a considerable distance from your present home and could lose sight of a CD or other IRA investment. It is imperative that you establish a recordkeeping system to keep track of your IRA investments, to check their yields, and in the case of your death, to assist your heirs in collecting benefits. Thus you should note these points:

1. When will you have to reinvest your fund? That is, when will your CD mature or your investment trust mature?

2. What are the penalties for terminating an investment before the end of a set term (bank penalties for premature with-

drawals; insurance company penalties for canceling an annuity)?

3. Who have you named as beneficiary and what payout methods have you selected?

Here is a form for keeping your IRA information in order. A separate form should be used for each investment.

Type of IRA _____ Account # _____

Trustee or custodian: _____

Address of trustee or custodian: _____

Beneficiary _____

Other information (Maturity date, interest rate, etc.) _____

_____

Date	Contribution	Earnings on contribution	Withdrawals	Balance

Chapter 4
YOUR SELF-EMPLOYMENT RETIREMENT PLAN

IF you are in business by yourself or in partnership with others and you want to provide for your retirement, the advantages of setting up a self-employed retirement or Keogh plan flow from:

1. Tax deductions claimed for contributions made to the plan;
2. Accumulations of tax-free income earned on assets held by the plan; and
3. Special averaging provisions for benefits paid on retirement.

To help you decide whether you should set up a Keogh plan, compare an estimate of the amount that a regular investment program would return to you on retirement with an estimate of the amount the Keogh plan would provide. If your comparison is based on a savings plan at a fixed rate of return, there is no question that the Keogh plan will give a greater return because of the tax benefits provided by the law. However, you should also consider these points before making your decision:

1. *Inclusion of permanent employees with service of at least three years.* You must include your employees in your Keogh plan and contribute funds for their retirement account. However, your contributions to their accounts are deductible, thus reducing the cost of your contribution.

If you have a large payroll, the cost of including your employees may eliminate the tax savings on your account. This possibility must be calculated in each case. The cost of including employees in a retirement plan may be balanced by increased goodwill.

2. *The amount of cash available for contributions.* After meeting both your personal and business expenses, do you have cash to put into the fund? You may solve part of this problem by providing that the plan has a variable formula of contributions to meet fluctuations in income.

3. *The availability of funds for emergencies.* The retirement fund is frozen until you reach age 59½, become disabled, or die. In case of financial emergency, your use of the fund may subject you to penalty tax.

The 1982 tax laws which generally take effect in 1984 will improve Keogh plan benefits. However, if you do not yet have a Keogh plan but are considering one for 1982 or 1983, you must familiarize yourself with the current rules.

Are you eligible to start a Keogh plan?

You may set up a Keogh plan if you earn self-employment income through your performance of personal services. For purposes of a Keogh plan, this income is called earned income and is your net profit (gross business or professional income less allowable business deductions). This income may be from your main occupation or from a sideline business. Income earned abroad and excluded from federal income tax is not considered earned income for purposes of the plan. If you are an inactive owner, such as a limited partner or a retired partner receiving distributions from the partnership, you may not make contributions to a Keogh plan.

An individual partner, although self-employed, may not set up a personal Keogh plan. The plan must be established by the partnership.

If you control more than one business (own more than 50% of the capital or profits interest in a partnership or the entire share of an unincorporated business), the following rules apply: (1) You must set up plans for all businesses under your control. These may be incorporated in one plan or remain separate. (2) Any additional plans must also conform to all regulations governing the original plan. (3) The additional plans must make contributions in an equal ratio and provide equal benefits.

These rules prevent you from increasing the maximum deductible contribution for your own benefit by contributing to more than one retirement plan. However, if you are an employee-member of a company retirement plan, you may set up a Keogh plan if you carry on a self-employed enterprise or profession on the side. For example, you are an attorney employed by a company that has a qualified pension plan of which you are a member. At the same time you have a practice on the side. You may set up a Keogh plan based on your self-employment earnings. Each plan is independent of the other.

A plan may not discriminate in terms of participation or benefits in favor of highly compensated personnel. Benefits must be for the employees and their beneficiaries, and their plan rights may not be subject to forfeiture. A plan may not allow any of its funds to be diverted for purposes other than pension benefits. Contributions made on your behalf may not exceed the ratio of contributions made on behalf of employees.

Choosing a plan

There are two general types of Keogh plans: defined-benefit plans and defined-contribution plans. A defined-benefit plan provides in advance for a specific retirement benefit funded by contributions based on an IRS formula and actuarial assumption. The basic benefit is computed on a percentage of pay or earned income up to $100,000. If your business has sufficient funds, a defined-benefit plan may, depending on your age and various actuarial assumptions, give you an opportunity to make deductible contributions in excess of $15,000 and to build up a larger retirement fund than possible through a defined-contribution plan. This plan has also been dubbed the "super-Keogh" because of the large contributions permitted under the plan. However, such a plan may prove costly if you have employees who also must be provided with proportionate defined benefits. Further, the plan requires you to contribute to their accounts even if you do not have profits.

Under a defined-contribution plan, retirement benefits will depend on the contributions made to your account and the accounts of your employees over the years the plan is in force. If contributions are geared to profits, the plan is a profit-sharing plan. If contributions are not based on the profits, the plan is a money-purchase pension plan; for example, a plan which provides that contributions to employees' accounts are to be based on a percentage of their pay is a money-purchase pension plan. If you set up such a plan, you must contribute to their accounts even though you do not have earnings and are not permitted to contribute to your account. On the other hand if the contribution formula to both your account and the account of your employees is based on earning profits, you make contributions to your account and your employees' accounts only in profitable years. In a loss year you are not required to make contributions.

If you set up a profit-sharing plan which includes employees, you must have a definite formula for determining contributions for them. The plan also must define the profits to be shared. Payments may be geared to profits on a graduated scale, such as on a stated percentage of profits. There is no definite formula if the plan lets the employers vary the percentage of profits paid each year. A payment formula is definite if it limits the amount for employees to the same percentage of compensation as the maximum percentage of earned income that may be contributed for your account. You may not amend a definite-payment formula except for valid business reasons. Beginning in 1984, however, the definite-formula requirement is eliminated.

Choosing the funding structure for your Keogh plan

You must formally set up your plan in writing on or before the end of the taxable year in which you want the plan to be effective.

If you are interested in following an aggressive investment policy for funds in your Keogh plan, you will set up a trust to receive Keogh contributions. You must name an independent trustee. As an owner-employee, you may not name yourself trustee until after 1983 when a new law becomes effective. However, you may reserve the right to give investment advice to the trustee concerning securities, real estate, and other investments.

As an owner-employee, you may appoint a bank or trust

company as the trustee. If the only investments of the trust are annuity, endowment, or life insurance contracts issued by a life insurance company with all proceeds payable directly to the employee (or his or her beneficiary), an individual may serve as trustee. The plan must state that a bank (or trust company) will be substituted as trustee if the IRS decides that the individual trustee is not keeping adequate records or filing adequate plan records.

In a partnership in which no partner owns more than a 10% interest, any qualified individual can be appointed trustee whether or not investments are limited to annuity, endowment, and life insurance policies.

Although as an owner-employee you may give investment directions to the trustee, you are prohibited from dealing with the trust if you own more than 50% of the business individually or with other owner-employees. You may not borrow from the trust. You may not buy property from or sell property to the trust; you may not charge any fees for services you render to the trust. These prohibitions also apply to any member of your immediate family, and any corporation in which you own more than half the voting stock, directly or indirectly. If you violate these rules, you are subject to penalties.

If you are considering an investment in saving certificates, you need not set up a trust; you may use a custodial account with the bank.

If you use funds to buy nontransferable annuity contracts from an insurance company, no trust may be necessary. Premium payments are made directly to the insurance company. The annuity contract may pay a fixed monthly income for life, or a fixed period of years, or may be a variable annuity contract.

Face-amount certificates may be bought directly from an insurance company and are considered annuity contracts. The certificates must not be transferable when held by anyone other than a trustee. The certificate or contract must state that it is not transferable. When a group certificate or contract is bought, the participants' interests must not be transferable. A certificate or contract is transferable if the owner can transfer any part of the interest in it to anyone other than the issuer. An employee may designate a beneficiary or choose any settlement under the plan.

Defined-contribution limitations

In 1982 and 1983 you may contribute and deduct up to 15% of your earned income or $15,000, whichever is less, to a defined-contribution plan. For self-employment tax purposes, earned income generally has the same meaning as net earnings from self-employment. Earned income is figured without regard to pension plan contributions. Beginning in 1984, however, earned income for purposes of figuring contributions is first reduced by deductible contributions on behalf of employees.

EXAMPLE—

A broker has net commission income of $24,000; his earned income is considered $24,000. He may contribute and deduct up to 15% of this amount, or $3600.

Foreign earned income, which is excluded from income tax, may not be counted as earned income even though it is subject to self-employment tax.

$200,000 compensation limit. To prevent a plan from discriminating against employees, the percentage limit may be computed on only the first $200,000 of annual compensation. However, if you earn more than $100,000, you will have to contribute at a rate of at least 7½% on behalf of your employees to take the full $15,000 deduction. The maximum compensation rule applies only through 1983; in 1984 and thereafter all self-employment income may be taken into account because new rules for top-heavy plans will prevent discrimination in favor of owners and other executives.

Minimum deduction if your adjusted gross income does not exceed $15,000. If your self-employment income is $750 to $5000 in a taxable year, and your adjusted gross income is $15,000 or less, you may deduct up to $750 in contributions even though this exceeds 15% of earned income. If you earn less than $750, you may deduct contributions up to 100% of your earned income.

In applying the $15,000 gross income test, only the self-employed's income is considered. The test is applied separately for each person claiming the deduction, and in a community-property state community-property laws are ignored in determining adjusted gross income. Adjusted gross income is determined *before* the deduction for Keogh plan contributions. The minimum deduction option is only available through 1983.

State law. The maximum contribution deductions allowed for federal income tax purposes do not necessarily apply for state income tax purposes. Some states still limit the deduction to the pre-1974 maximum deduction of $2500; other states require income adjustments.

Contribution limits beginning in 1984. The limitation on Keogh plan contributions at the lesser of $15,000 or 15% of earned income will not apply after December 31, 1983. The maximum contribution limit increases and will be the same as for corporate defined-contribution plans: the lesser of 25% of earned income or $30,000. There is no minimum contribution option.

Defined-benefit contribution limitations

A defined-benefit plan allows you to build up retirement benefits equal to a percentage of your earnings. In 1982 and 1983 the percentage is computed under an IRS formula according to age and is applied to your earnings. For example, your earnings in 1982 are $80,000 and you are 50 years of age, and you start a plan in 1982. An IRS percentage of 3% for your age would give a benefit credit of $2400. Assuming that your earnings remained constant at $80,000 until age 65, your annual retirement benefit under the IRS formula would be $36,000 (15 years × $2400). To determine the actual amount to be contributed each year to fund the annual $36,000 payment you need a computation from an actuary. The amount of the annual contribution determined by the actuary may exceed the amount regularly allowed under the defined-contribution rule but is subject to the overall limit applied to corporate defined-benefit plans (see Chapter 5).

The IRS has released model defined plans which take into

consideration all the technical rules applied to defined-benefit plans. Contributions may be placed in a trust or used to purchase annuity contracts from an insurance company.

IRS regulations provide for two types of defined-benefit plans: final average pay plans and career average pay plans. A final average pay plan accrues benefits based on compensation over a period less than the total participation period, for example, during the last four years of participation. Career average pay plans accrue benefits based on all years of participation.

The maximum benefit for a career average pay plan is determined by your annual compensation and an applicable percentage fixed in the year participation begins. If a career average pay plan is noncontributory and provides no benefits other than a straight-life annuity commencing at the later of age 65 or the day five years after the day the participant's current period of participation began, the maximum basic benefit for each year of plan participation equals compensation for that year (not exceeding $100,000), multiplied by one of the following percentages:

Age when participation begins	Percentage
30 or less	6.5
35	5.4
40	4.4
45	3.6
50	3.0
55	2.5
60 or over	2.0

The percentage stays the same for each year, as long as participation in the plan is continuous. Thus the maximum benefit that could be accrued for the first plan year by a 30-year-old employee earning $30,000 is $1950 (6.5% of $30,000). If in the second plan year the employee's compensation increases to $35,000, the maximum benefit that could be accrued for that year is $2275 (6.5% of $35,000).

If a career average pay plan offers benefits other than a straight-life annuity, such as a joint and survivor annuity for married employees, disability benefits, or benefits that vary according to the cost of living, the percentages in the above table must be adjusted. The IRS will provide the adjustment factor.

Past service credits are not considered in determining the age at which a self-employed individual's period of participation in the plan began. If an employee is covered by a plan, leaves the plan after a few years, and then recommences participation at a later date, a different percentage is used for each period of plan participation.

EXAMPLE—

A self-employed person first participates in a defined-benefit plan at age 30. He leaves the plan at age 35 but rejoins at age 50.

If his covered pay is as listed below, his maximum retirement benefit per year of $24,500 is computed as follows:

Age	Compensation per year	Rate	Benefit earned per year	Total benefit
30–35	$20,000	6.5	$1300 (× 5)	$ 6,500
50–55	30,000	3.0	900 (× 5)	4,500
55–60	40,000	3.0	1200 (× 5)	6,000
60–65	50,000	3.0	1500 (× 5)	7,500
	Total			$24,500

The actual annual contributions to fund this plan would be determined by an actuary.

Rules for determining benefit accruals under final average pay plans are even more complex than those outlined above for career average pay plans. The Treasury provides a worksheet in its regulations for calculating the maximum benefit under final average pay plans.

You may not take advantage of a defined-benefit plan unless it provides benefits for all your employees without taking into account benefits under Social Security. All plans of a controlled group of businesses are aggregated for purposes of the limitations applied to defined benefits.

To assure reasonable comparability between defined benefit and defined contribution and combinations of plans, the regulations provide for appropriate adjustments in the allowable amount of deductible contributions, or permissible rate of benefit accruals in cases where the same self-employed individual is a participant in two or more plans.

Important: The above discussion is a general outline of defined-benefit plans. Other technical rules are complex and their implementation requires the services of an expert who can design a plan to fit your circumstances.

After 1983 the present limitations on defined-benefit Keogh plans no longer apply. The special percentage and the maximum earnings that can be taken into account ($200,000) for figuring Keogh plan benefits under a defined-benefit plan apply only through 1983. Thereafter the same limitations as for corporate benefits apply: the maximum benefit is the lesser of $90,000 or 100% of average compensation for your three consecutive highest earning years.

When to make annual contributions

Contributions may be made until the due date for your tax return (plus extensions). Thus contributions for 1982 may be made at any time during 1982 and until April 15, 1983. However, a written plan must be set up no later than the end of the year. If you are on a calendar year and have not established your Keogh plan by December 31, you may not contribute to it for that year.

While it is advantageous to make contributions as early as possible to permit earnings to accumulate tax free, as a practical matter you may be forced to delay making contributions until the end of the year. This will allow you to figure your earnings, the compensation of your employees upon which contributions will be based, and in the case of a profit-sharing plan, your profits.

Including employees in your plan

In 1982 and 1983 you must provide retirement benefits for *all* your employees who are 25 years old or older and have at least three years' service. A year's service is a 12-month period starting from the date work begins and during which at least 1000 hours of service is completed. This works out to about 30 weeks of employment at 35 hours per week. Therefore you do not have to include part-time or seasonal workers.

Once an employee is included in your plan, benefits must vest immediately. Thus an employee has a nonforfeitable right to benefits from your contribution.

You may shorten or waive the three-year period as long as you do so for all employees and not just for one or a few. If an owner-employee with less than three years of service participates in the plan, the shorter service requirement must apply to all employees. Similarly, if credit is granted to an owner-employee for prior service in a former partnership, employees must be granted similar credit if applicable.

You may not exclude an employee because he or she is too old. However, if you have a defined-benefit Keogh plan, you do not have to include an employee who starts employment within five years of normal retirement age as set forth in the plan.

Beginning in 1984 a Keogh plan is not required to include employees and vest benefits under the rules outlined above. It may follow the same rules as corporate plans and adopt any permissible vesting schedule. However, if your plan is considered top heavy because it disproportionately benefits you, other owners, and key personnel (explained in Chapter 5), you must adopt a stricter vesting schedule.

If you have a profit-sharing plan in 1982 or 1983, you must set a definite formula under which you will make contributions on behalf of employees. The plan must define "profits" for purposes of the formula. The percentage of profits contributed may not be varied at the discretion of the owner-employee. After 1983 the definite formula requirement is eliminated. You may coordinate the plan with Social Security. That is, under certain conditions your payments can take into account Social Security taxes which you pay for the employees and so reduce the cost of your contributions. This is called integration. A defined-benefit plan may not be integrated with Social Security. Beginning in 1984 the tax rate for the old-age, survivors, and disability insurance (OASDI) portion of FICA is the maximum rate at which contributions may be reduced under integrated plans. Congressional committee reports give this example: Based on the 1982 OASDI tax rate of 5.4% and the 1982 wage base of $32,400, a profit-sharing plan could provide no contributions for the first $32,400 of pay and make contributions equal to 5.4% of pay in excess of $32,400. If larger contributions, such as 10%, were desired for pay over $32,400, contributions of at least 4.6% (10% − 5.4%) must be made for the first $32,400 in order to integrate the plan with Social Security.

You must furnish to your employees written notice of the plan, including a description of its features.

Your contributions on behalf of your employees are deductible.

Voluntary contributions may allow for increased tax-free accumulations

You may set up a plan which permits you and your employees to make additional *voluntary* contributions to your account and to theirs. Contributions may be up to 10% of their pay. You and your employees may not deduct such contributions, but there is an advantage to making voluntary contributions: earnings on the fund accumulate without tax.

If you allow your employees to make voluntary contributions, you too may make an additional contribution in the same proportion as your employees. The additional contribution may not exceed 10% of earned income or $2500, whichever is less. If you are covered by more than one retirement plan, your total voluntary contributions may not exceed $2500 per year.

A plan covering only self-employed persons may not allow for voluntary contributions.

Important: Beginning in 1984 the limit on voluntary contributions for owners is repealed. Contributions above deduction limitations are not subject to the penalty tax, and earnings on the contributions may accumulate tax free.

When can you receive retirement benefits?

As a self-employed person you may not receive benefits from the plan before the taxable year in which you reach age 59½ or are totally disabled prior to that time. You are considered disabled if you cannot engage in substantial gainful activity because of an illness that can be expected to be of long and indefinite duration or to result in death.

Your entire interest must be paid to you (1) no later than the taxable year in which you are age 70½ or retire, or (2) a period not extending beyond your life expectancy or the life expectancy of you and your spouse, provided that the distributions begin no later than the taxable year in which you are age 70½ or retire. However, beginning in 1984, if your plan is top heavy, distributions must begin by the year in which you reach age 70½ even if you do not retire.

Your plan must provide for the restriction of payments of benefits before age 59½, except for disability (explained later in this chapter) or death. This restriction applies even if the plan is terminated.

Voluntary contributions (nondeductible contributions, if permitted) made after September 2, 1974, may be withdrawn at any time without regard to the age restriction.

Until 1984 there is no minimum age at which benefits for employees may be received. However, an employee's benefits must begin no later than 60 days after the taxable year in which the latest of these events occurs: the employee reaches normal retirement age, as established by the plan; terminates employment; or completes ten years of participation in the plan. In 1984 a minimum age distribution is imposed which is the later of the year in which an employee reaches age 70½ or retires.

Payments to beneficiaries. If you or an employee in your plan dies before all retirement benefits are paid, or payments are being made to a surviving spouse who dies before the entire interest is received, the balance must be paid within five years after death (or that of the surviving spouse) to the beneficiaries.

If death occurs after distributions have begun the five-year restrictions do not apply, provided the distributions were geared to the joint life expectancy of you and your spouse or your employee and his spouse.

Beginning in 1984 beneficiaries of owners will be entitled to claim the $5000 death benefit exclusion.

Incidental life insurance coverage

Some life insurance coverage may be purchased through a Keogh plan, provided it is considered incidental to the plan. In a defined-benefit plan funded with insurance contracts, the life insurance is considered incidental if it is not more than 100 times the monthly annuity, such as $1000 of life insurance for each $10 of monthly annuity. If a defined-contribution plan includes term life insurance, the premium may not be more than 25% of a contribution. If whole-life insurance is used and half of the premium is for insurance protection and half for a cash reserve, the limit is 50% of contributions.

While the limit on contributions to Keogh plans increases after 1983, the rules restricting payments for incidental life insurance coverage will still apply.

How benefits are taxed

The way benefits are paid, whether in a lump sum or as an annuity, determines how benefits will be taxed. The method of payment is usually provided in the plan. For example, if your Keogh plan invested in an annuity, you would receive annuity payments.

Lump-sum distributions. If you receive a lump-sum distribution, you may treat the portion attributable to pre-1974 years as long-term capital gain; the portion of a distribution allocable to 1974 and later years is taxable as ordinary income. To qualify for capital gain treatment you must elect to use the ten-year averaging computation for the ordinary income portion. To elect the ten-year averaging method you must have participated in the plan for at least five years. If your capital gains are taxed at a higher tax rate than that of the ten-year averaging method, you may forgo capital gain treatment and treat your entire distribution as ordinary income subject to the ten-year averaging method.

A lump-sum distribution may be rolled over to an IRA to avoid current taxation.

If you bought U.S. Retirement Bonds before May 1, 1982,

redemptions do not qualify for ten-year averaging or capital gain treatment even if redemption is in a lump sum. The proceeds from redemption are ordinary income to which you may apply the regular averaging method. The mere distribution of bonds is not a taxable event; taxation arises upon redemption of the bonds.

Annuity payments. These are taxable except for payments allocable to your investment in the policy. Your deductible contributions are not considered an investment in the policy. You have an investment if you made voluntary contributions.

Withholding on distributions. Generally, beginning on January 1, 1983, payors of pensions are required to withhold on distributions unless you elect otherwise. Withholding rules are discussed in Chapter 8.

Penalties

A Keogh plan entails certain reporting requirements. The failure to observe them may result in substantial penalties. Similarly, penalties are imposed for premature distributions and for excess contributions.

Penalty for failure to file report. The penalty for failing to file the annual comprehensive report is $10 a day until it is filed (maximum penalty $5000). The penalty will be waived upon a showing that the delay was due to reasonable cause.

Premature distributions. In 1982 and 1983, a 10% penalty is imposed on a premature distribution, that is, one made before you are age 59½, unless you become totally disabled.

A person is disabled if he or she is unable to engage in any substantial gainful activity because of a physical or mental condition which has lasted or is expected to last for a long period or is expected to lead to death. A condition that can be corrected is not a disability. The person is not considered disabled if, with reasonable effort and safety, the condition can be alleviated so that the person can hold a job.

For the first year in which a distribution is made you must attach to your return a doctor's statement explaining the effect of the mental or physical condition, why you are unable to continue working, and the date the condition began.

For distributions in later years you attach a statement saying that the condition has not lessened substantially and that it still prevents you from working.

Premature distributions are subject to the 10% income tax penalty in addition to the regular tax which results from including the distribution in income. The penalty may not be reduced by the investment credit or foreign tax credit; it also may not be considered in computing the minimum tax. You are also disqualified from having contributions made on your behalf for five years following the year of distribution, unless the distribution results from plan termination.

You are prohibited from borrowing from the plan. Borrowings are treated as taxable distributions. Previously, this rule applied only to partners owning more than a 10% partnership interest. Loans outstanding as of December 31, 1981, are not affected by this law change.

Also considered as premature distributions are pledges of your interest in the plan, a loan made by an insurance company under a contract purchased by the plan, and a payment of an overdue premium in the form of a loan against the cash surrender value of the contract.

The IRS has ruled that a tax-free rollover may be made if the Keogh plan is terminated. A timely rollover will avoid the 10% penalty on premature distributions if the recipient is under 59½.

Excess contributions. For 1982 and 1983 excess contributions are subject to a nondeductible 6% cumulative excise tax. For a defined-contribution plan excess contributions are generally amounts contributed in excess of the $15,000/15% ceiling. In a defined-benefit plan the penalty applies if the plan is fully funded at the close of the taxable year, and the tax is imposed on the amount that is not deductible for the year of contribution or any prior year. Voluntary contributions by self-employed individuals in excess of their allowable amounts are also treated as excess contributions. The owner-employee who maintains the plan is liable for the tax.

A repayment of the excess contributions or a "correcting distribution" may stop the running of the penalty. Contributions above the ceiling on allowable contributions may be withdrawn without penalty provided no deduction is taken for the excess contributions, the withdrawal is made before the due date for the tax return, and any income earned on the excess contribution is included in income.

The excess contribution penalty is repealed in 1984.

How to qualify your plan

You may set up your plan and contribute to it without advance IRS approval. As a practical matter, advance approval is advisable to avoid disqualification at some later date. Thus you may ask the district director for the district in which your business is located to review your plan. If you are setting up a trust you will need to consult an attorney versed in the field to prepare the trust agreement and to submit a request for IRS approval.

If you join a master or prototype plan, plan approval is simple. The sponsoring organization submits to the IRS Form 3672 for a defined-contribution plan or Form 3672A for a defined-benefit plan. When the master or prototype is approved, a number is assigned to the plan. The sponsoring organization then advises participating employers of the full name of the plan, the date of the favorable opinion letter, and the plan number.

Amendments to plans to conform them to changes in the law, such as the 1982 increase in the maximum contribution from $7500 to $15,000, do not generally require determination letters or opinion letters. Be sure to have existing plans reviewed and updated to reflect changes made by the 1982 Tax Act.

Deducting costs of a plan

Fees charged for setting up a Keogh plan are deductible as ordinary business expenses. If possible, pay trustee and actuary fees directly from your business rather than through plan contributions.

Liberalized Keogh plan rules for large partnerships

If you have a partnership in which no one partner owns more than 10% of the capital interest or 10% of the profits of the partnership, you may set up a Keogh plan in 1982 or 1983 free of the restrictions placed on owner-employees. For example, in a partnership of 20 individuals each of whom owns an equal share of the capital and profits, there are no owner-employees; each owns only a 5% interest. Thus the partnership may set up a Keogh plan that more closely resembles a corporate plan than the plan of an owner-employee. Beginning in 1984 there are no longer special restrictions for plans with owner-employees. Thus there is no distinction for Keogh plans of large partnerships.

A plan without an owner-employee may use as its trustee a partner or any other qualified person or institution. The trustee is not required to be a bank or other institution as in the case of an owner-employee plan.

Immediate vesting of benefits or contributions made on behalf of employees other than owner-employees is not required in a plan where there are no owner-employees. The plan may adopt any vesting schedule within the parameters of vesting requirements for qualified plans as explained in Chapter 5.

While the deduction limitations are the same for plans with or without owner-employees, there are no special contribution limits on behalf of persons owning less than 10%. Thus there is the opportunity to accumulate larger retirement funds through tax-free compounding.

A plan in which there are no owner-employees does not have to restrict distributions before age 59½ or require distributions by age 70½. Instead the plan must provide that benefits will be paid on the later of reaching age 70½ or retirement. The plan may provide for early retirement before age 59½.

A profit-sharing plan in which there are no owner-employees need not have a definite formula for the amount of profits to be shared by employees.

A pension plan in which there are no owner-employees may

integrate Social Security benefits along with retirement benefits under the same rules applied to corporate plans as discussed in Chapter 5. This greatly reduces the cost of contributions. Owner-employee defined-benefit plans may be integrated, but special rules apply.

Chapter 5
YOUR CORPORATE RETIREMENT PLAN

Setting up a qualified company retirement plan

IF you have incorporated your business, setting up a qualified company retirement plan makes sound tax and investment sense. Your company receives a current deduction for contributions made to the plan, and you and other covered employees are not taxed on company contributions. Income earned on the contributions accumulates tax free. Tax is incurred when benefits are received. The results of tax-free compounding are illustrated in Chapter 2.

If you have employees, you must balance your personal benefits against the cost of including employees in the plan. A plan cannot qualify unless it provides for full-time employees. Further, starting in 1984 top-heavy plans which favor stockholders or highly paid executives will have to pay minimum benefits to other employees. Against the cost of covering employees, consider the goodwill created by providing employee benefits. In addition to contribution costs you must also consider the costs of plan administration, which may be substantial, in your decision to set up a retirement plan.

When setting up a company plan, these important decisions must be made:

1. What type of retirement plan should I select: a pension plan or a deferred profit-sharing plan?
2. How much will the company contribute to the plan?
3. Should the plan allow for voluntary contributions?
4. When will employees be permitted to enter the plan?
5. When will employee benefits vest?

6. What happens to benefits when an employee terminates employment?
7. When must employees retire?

This chapter explains the kinds of company retirement plans, options you may select, and procedures you must follow. As a general observation, the laws governing pension plans are extremely technical, and you should consult an expert in the field before establishing a retirement program.

Changes introduced by the 1982 Tax Act have generally reduced the benefits available under corporate plans, and starting in 1984 there will be parity between the benefits available under corporate retirement plans and plans of the self-employed. Thus after 1983 there will no longer be an incentive to incorporate in order to obtain retirement benefit advantages. Review your plan with your pension consultant to determine the implications and impact of the new law changes.

Should you start a pension or profit-sharing plan?

Only a qualified retirement plan enjoys tax deductions for contributions, tax-free accumulations of income, and special tax treatment for distributions. A qualified plan is one that the IRS approves as having met certain standards concerning eligibility, benefits, and reporting.

A corporation may choose from several types of qualified retirement plans: pension plan, profit-sharing plan, stock-bonus plan, thrift plan, or a combination of plans. In general, only pension and profit-sharing plans are discussed in this book.

A pension plan is designed to provide a fixed benefit upon retirement. There are two types of pension plans. In a defined-benefit plan, the level of benefits is fixed and contributions are geared to provide those benefits at retirement. In a defined-contribution plan, it is the contributions that are fixed, and benefits depend on the size of the contributions and the number of years before retirement. Both types of pension plans differ from profit-sharing plans in that contributions must be made, regardless of profits.

If your corporation chooses a defined-benefit plan, the first step is deciding on a formula for determining benefits. Benefits are often based on years of service and a percentage of earnings over a certain period. For example, a plan may provide for a pension equal to a small percentage (1% or 2%) of an employee's average compensation during the last five years before retirement multiplied by years of service. For high earners, the pension allowed by the plan may have to be reduced because the law limits the annual benefit payable by defined-benefit plans, discussed below.

Once the benefit formula is determined, the company will actuarially compute the level of contributions needed to provide the funds to pay the anticipated benefits. Contributions must be made, regardless of profits. To determine annual contributions, an actuary will consider your age, earnings, and years before reaching retirement. Earnings of the fund may also affect contributions. If the fund earns more than the rate assumed when the plan was set up, the company may decrease its contributions; the IRS could require increased contributions if the plan did not earn as much as had been assumed.

In a defined-contribution plan, such as a money-purchase pension plan, the company commits itself to make a fixed annual contribution, regardless of profits. For example, a money-purchase plan may require contributions equal to 10% of each participant's annual salary. Contributions plus earnings on the fund will determine benefits.

In general, the money-purchase plan is favored if the employees are relatively young, since retirement benefits depend on the number of years they are in the plan. Older employees with fewer years until retirement prefer a defined-benefit plan which can set benefits at the maximum allowed by law.

Unlike a pension plan, a profit-sharing plan does not have fixed benefits. Contributions are made out of corporate profits and allocated to the employees participating in the plan according to a definite formula. The allocation must not discriminate in favor of stockholders, officers, and executives. At retirement or other payout date (upon disability, for example), the employee receives the amount allocated to his or her account plus the income and capital appreciation attributable to the allocated amount. A profit-sharing plan is a type of defined-contribution plan. The contribution is limited by a written formula;

retirement benefits will be whatever the accumulated amount of contributions can buy upon retirement.

A pension plan should be considered only if the earnings record of your business shows a reasonable amount of stability. Pension plans call for regular contributions by your company, regardless of profits. A pension plan must be actuarially sound; the contributions must be sufficient to pay a fixed monthly sum to an employee who reaches retirement age and retires. To meet this obligation, the law imposes minimum standards; contributions are figured accordingly.

A profit-sharing plan is more flexible since your company is not obligated to pay a fixed annual amount into the fund. It may contribute according to a formula keyed to profits. In loss years it may contribute nothing, while in prosperous years contributions can be substantial. Profit-sharing plans furnish employee incentives to increase profits, whereas pension plans furnish the employee security through fixed and prearranged future benefits.

The selection of a particular plan depends on your projection of future business conditions. Other factors to be weighed are the rate of labor turnover, the ratio of young to older employees, and the tax burden. Pension plans favor older employees; profit-sharing plans favor younger employees.

Pension plans are more costly to administer. In addition to fees for actuarial computations, you are required to pay premiums to the Pension Benefit Guaranty Corporation on behalf of each employee covered by a pension plan. The annual premium is currently $2.60 per covered employee. Premiums are designed to cover retirement benefits for plans that fail or are terminated before benefits are fully funded.

Pension plans and profit-sharing plans must provide for a trustee, except in the case of an annuity pension plan in which contracts are bought from an insurance company. If you set up a pension plan and fund it by buying an annuity contract, you give up all control over the investment of plan funds. The insurance company handles the investments and guarantees payment of stipulated benefits.

If you use a trustee plan, your plan involves the creation of a trust which is responsible for the investment and payment of funds contributed to it. You may name yourself trustee and you will be subject to fiduciary responsibility rules.

Overall limits on retirement contributions and benefits

New and existing company plans have to take into account the 1982 law changes in figuring the maximum benefits that may be provided under a pension or profit-sharing plan.

Defined-benefit plans. In 1982 the highest annual benefit which may be paid by a defined-benefit pension plan is the lower of $136,425 or 100% of an employee's average pay for the highest three consecutive calendar years he or she was an active participant. The $136,425 dollar limitation includes a cost-of-living adjustment. After 1982 the dollar limitation on annual benefits decreases from $136,425 to $90,000. The $90,000 limit will apply if it is less than the percentage limitation, which has not been changed—100% of average compensation for the employee's highest three consecutive earning years. If benefits are not paid in the form of a straight-life annuity, such as when a lump-sum distribution is made, the benefit must be made actuarially equivalent to the defined-benefit limitations by assuming an interest rate of at least 5%.

Existing defined-benefit pension plans will generally be subject to the $90,000 overall benefit limitation after December 31, 1982. In years beginning after 1982 you will not be able to deduct more than the amount of contributions needed to fund the annual benefit under the $90,000/100% of average pay ceiling. However, those who were already accruing benefits in excess of $90,000 before 1983 will not be adversely affected; they may continue to apply the old $136,425 limit. A plan in existence on July 1, 1982 does not have to be amended immediately; no plan will be disqualified for years beginning before January 1, 1984 if it provides for maximum benefits which exceed the post-1982 overall limits, as long as the pre-1983 maximums are not violated. Plan amendments will have to be made by the last day of the first plan year beginning after December 31, 1983. Plans which were not established until after July 1,

1982 have to comply with the lower $90,000 limitation immediately.

The $90,000 benefit limit for defined-benefit plans assumes retirement at age 65. If retirement occurs earlier or later than age 65, benefits will have to be refigured. The $90,000 limit for defined-benefit plans must be actuarially reduced using an interest rate of at least 5% for employees retiring before age 62. For retirement benefits paid at or before age 55, the maximum dollar limit may not be less than the actuarial equivalent of a $75,000 annual benefit commencing at age 55. If retirement benefits do not begin until after age 65, the $90,000 defined-benefit limit must be actuarially increased to the equivalent of a benefit beginning at age 65.

Cost-of-living adjustments to the $90,000 defined-benefit limitation will not be allowed until 1986 when the limit will be adjusted for post-1984 cost-of-living increases.

Profit-sharing plan. There is no absolute restriction on benefits, but as a practical matter benefits are limited since there is a ceiling on the amount which may be contributed annually on behalf of each participating employee. In a profit-sharing plan, participating employees may also make voluntary contributions which are not forfeitable. Company contributions may be determined each year by separate action of the board of directors or by a contribution formula written in the trust agreement. Examples of contribution formulas:

1. The company agrees to contribute a flat percentage of profits.
2. The company agrees to contribute a percentage of profits above a set minimum.
3. The company agrees to increase the percentage as profits increase; 10% for the first $25,000 of profits; 20% for profits between $25,000 and $50,000; 30% for profits over $50,000.

In 1982 the maximum amount which may be contributed annually to an employee's profit-sharing account is the lower of 25% of compensation or $45,475, which includes a cost-of-living adjustment. However, in years beginning after 1982 the dollar limit for annual additions to an employee's account under a profit-sharing plan is reduced from $45,475 to $30,000.

This $30,000 limit will apply if it is less than the percentage limitation of 25% of compensation. Cost-of-living increases to the $30,000 dollar limitation will not be allowed until 1986.

The reduced dollar limit for contributions to profit-sharing plans takes effect in 1983 and therefore governs 1983 deductions for contributions, although an existing plan does not have to be amended until plan years beginning after 1983.

The following amounts are subject to the $30,000/25% pay ceiling: employer contributions, forfeitures credited to the employee, and the lesser of (1) one-half of the employee's contribution, or (2) employee contributions in excess of 6% of compensation. Employee rollovers are not included. If an employer maintains more than one plan, the $30,000/25% limit applies to the total additions to all plans.

The $30,000/25% ceiling on annual additions will also apply after 1982 to defined-contribution pension plans, such as money-purchase plans, which contribute a fixed amount each year, regardless of profits.

For plan years beginning after December 31, 1981, you may make deductible contributions to a profit-sharing or other defined-contribution plan on behalf of permanently and totally disabled employees other than officers, owners, or highly compensated individuals. Contributions are based on the employee's compensation immediately prior to becoming disabled. The contributions must be nonforfeitable to be deductible.

Multiple plans. An employer is not limited to one plan. There may be, for example, two pension plans or one pension plan and one profit-sharing plan. However, multiple plans may not be used to exceed the contribution limit. The law requires that all the plans of an employer be aggregated to test contribution limitations.

If an employer maintains two or more similar plans (e.g., two profit-sharing plans), they are treated as one plan and total contributions may not exceed the limit for one plan. If an employer maintains two or more dissimilar plans (a pension plan and a profit-sharing plan), special limitations apply. A formula is applied on a per-employee basis each year so that total contributions and benefits stay within certain limits. The formula is the total of a defined-benefit fraction and a defined-contribution fraction. These fractions are quite complex and special elections are available. The services of a retirement expert are needed to assure compliance with the aggregate limits.

For 1982 the total of the two fractions can not exceed 1.4 (140%); otherwise, one or all of the plans could be disqualified. For years after 1982 more complicated limitations will apply. Generally, the sum of the two fractions is limited after 1982 to the lesser of 1.4 or 1.25 times the dollar limitations. Starting in 1984 there is a further limitation for key employees who participate in a defined-benefit plan and defined-contribution plan included in a top-heavy group. (Top-heavy plans are discussed later in this chapter.) The aggregate limit on benefits and contributions for key employees under the defined-benefit and contribution fractions will generally be the lesser of 1.4 or 1.0 times the dollar limits. The 1.0 limit may be increased to the regular 1.25 limit for multiple plans if certain additional tests are satisfied.

Covering employees

An owner may not set up a qualified plan solely for personal benefit. To obtain the benefits of a retirement plan, employees must be entitled to approximately the same benefits. However, this does not mean that a $10,000-a-year employee will receive the same retirement benefits as one earning $50,000. It means only that if each has been with the company the same length of time, they are both eligible to participate in the plan.

You can require that a new employee work for a specified length of time and reach a certain age before he or she is eligible to participate in the plan. However, you may not exclude an employee who has reached age 25 if he or she has at least one year of service. If your plan provides for full and immediate vesting of an employee's benefits, an employee may be required to complete a maximum of three years of service before participating. You need not cover seasonal or part-time employees who work less than 1000 hours during a 12-month period.

If you set up a defined-benefit pension plan you can exclude an employee who is within five years of normal retirement age (which may not be later than age 65) when his or her period of service begins. For example, an employee hired at age 62 does not have to be included in the plan. This exclusion is not considered an act of age discrimination. A plan may also provide that no benefits are to be paid a participant until the tenth anniversary of the date the period of service began. There can be no maximum age restriction for participation in a money-purchase pension plan or profit-sharing plan.

When you set up a company plan, you must notify your employees of its existence. Failure to do so disqualifies the plan. This can be done by a letter directed to all employees telling them of the adoption of the plan by the board of directors. Once employees become plan participants, further disclosure is required. Within 90 days of beginning participation, employees must receive a description of the plan. Each year they must also receive a copy of the latest annual report. When an employee terminates employment, a statement concerning vested benefits must be supplied. An employee may request a statement concerning the amount of benefits and when they will vest; the request must be in writing.

Integrating a pension or profit-sharing plan with Social Security

To the extent that employees are covered by Social Security, an employer may reduce its obligation to fund their retirement benefits. By paying a part of the employees' FICA taxes, an employer is considered to have already funded part of their retirement benefits through Social Security. When setting up a company plan, you may decide whether to take into account Social Security benefits payable to employees. You do not have to consider Social Security benefits, but if you do the IRS requires that specific tests be met to assure that the combined benefits or contributions under the plan and Social Security do not discriminate in favor of officers, stockholders, or highly paid employees. The integration rules are complex and depend on whether the company plan is a defined-benefit plan or a defined-contribution plan. These rules are set out in Treasury regulations and rulings. For example, a defined-benefit company plan may be an "offset plan" in which the total benefits called for under the plan are offset by the employees' Social Security benefits. A defined-benefit plan may be an "excess plan" in which company benefits are based only on income above a specified level. Treasury rules provide special tables for integrating such plans with Social Security.

Defined-contribution plans, such as profit-sharing plans and money-purchase pension plans, may also be integrated with Social Security by taking into account contributions rather than benefits. Here, too, rules for determining the integration level and company contributions are in Treasury regulations.

After 1983 a new requirement will govern integration of profit-sharing and other defined-contribution plans with Social Security. For plan years beginning after December 31, 1983, company contributions may be reduced by no more than the employer tax rate for old-age, survivors, and disability insurance (OASDI). The exact figures will depend on the Social Security wage base and OASDI tax rate for the particular year. Committee reports give this example: Based on the 1982 employer's tax rate of 5.4% for OASDI benefits and the 1982 wage base of $32,400, a profit-sharing plan could provide no contributions for the first $32,400 of pay and make contributions equal to 5.4% of pay in excess of $32,400. If an employer wants to contribute 10% of pay over $32,400, contributions of at least 4.6% (10% − 5.4%) would have to be made for the first $32,400 in order to integrate the plan with Social Security.

When employee benefits must vest

For a qualified plan, the law imposes vesting rules to ensure that, at a definite time, all or part of an employee's benefits become nonforfeitable. A plan may adopt one of three vesting schedules:

1. 100% vesting after ten years;
2. 25% vesting after five years, 5% each year thereafter, up to 50% after ten years, and 10% each year thereafter, up to 100% after 15 years; or
3. Rule of 45, which requires that an employee's benefits must be 50% vested when his or her age and years of service together total 45 or after ten years of service, whichever occurs first with an additional 10% vesting for each additional year of service thereafter.

The IRS may require vesting over a shorter period if faster vesting is needed to prevent discrimination in favor of officers, stockholders, and highly paid employees.

The minimum vesting schedules apply to both pension and profit-sharing plans.

Regardless of the rule used, retirement benefits from employer contributions must be at least 50% vested when the employee has ten years of service.

Vesting rules for top-heavy plans after 1983. For years in which a plan is top heavy as explained in the following pages, one of two vesting schedules will have to be met: (1) employees with three years of service have a nonforfeitable right to 100% of their accrued benefits from employer contributions, or (2) employee benefits are 100% vested after six years under a graded vesting schedule based on years of service, as follows:

Years of service	Amount vested
2	20%
3	40%
4	60%
5	80%
6 and more	100%

Benefits after 1983 under top-heavy plans

Starting in 1984 plans that disproportionately favor owners and other key employees will be subject to special rules to protect all employees in the plan. Such plans are called top-heavy plans.

A profit-sharing or other defined-contribution plan will be considered a top-heavy plan for the plan year if the account balances for "key employees" exceed 60% of the account balances for all employees. A defined-benefit plan will be considered a top-heavy plan for a plan year if the present value of the accrued benefits for "key employees" exceeds 60% of the value of the total accrued benefits for all employees. Whether a plan is top heavy is a determination made each year. The determination date is the last day of the preceding plan year (or in the case of a new plan, the last day of the first plan year). In figuring an employee's account, distributions within five years of the determination date are taken into account. However, a rollover contribution after 1983 is not figured into the employee's account unless the rollover was between plans of the same employer.

Key employees include officers (up to 50), a more than 5% owner, a more than 1% owner with compensation over $150,000, and employees with the ten largest ownership interests. Further, an individual who was an officer or owner within the four preceding years is considered a key employee. Stock owned by family members will be attributed to employees under the constructive ownership rules.

If a single employer has more than one plan covering key employees, the top-heavy rules apply to the aggregated group. Plans of related employers may also be aggregated under this test.

If a plan is top heavy under the above rules it will be able to take into account only the first $200,000 of employee compensation in determining contributions or benefits. Starting in 1986 the $200,000 limit may be increased for post-1984 cost-of-living increases. Further, there is a special limitation on the aggregate contributions and benefits for key employees under multiple plans, as noted above.

Top-heavy plans will have to provide minimum contributions or benefits to employees who are not key employees. Generally, the minimum benefit under a defined-benefit plan will be the lesser of (1) 2% of average pay in the five highest consecutive earning years times years of service, or (2) 20% of such average pay. In figuring minimum benefits, years of service completed in plan years beginning before 1984 are disregarded; also disregarded are years of service in years for which plans are not top heavy. For a defined-contribution plan, the minimum contribution for non-key employees would generally be 3% of compensation or, if lower, the contribution rate for the highest paid key employee would apply. Social Security benefits may not be taken into account in figuring required minimum benefits or contributions.

Distributions to key employees. A 10% premature withdrawal penalty will apply to distributions after 1983 to key employees from top-heavy plans prior to age 59½. The penalty will not apply to distributions made because of the employee's disability or death. Further, a top-heavy plan will have to commence retirement distributions to key employees by the year in which they reach age 70½, even if they do not retire.

How much is deductible?

The corporation may claim a tax deduction for its contributions. The maximum amount of the deduction is determined by the type of plan it has set up. Limitations vary between pension or profit-sharing plans.

If your company uses an insurance company with which to fund your pension plan, it may deduct premiums charged by the insurance company which are based on reasonable actuarial assumptions and on a rigid premium structure. The premiums must be paid to the insurance company directly or through a trust; the benefits must not anticipate future increases in compensation.

Profit-sharing plan. The basic limitation on deductions to a profit-sharing plan or trust for a taxable year is 15% of the annual compensation of the covered employees. If the amount contributed to the plan is more than the deductible amount (15% of compensation), a contribution carryover is allowed. The excess contributions are deductible only in a later year when contributions are less than that year's 15% limitation. The carryover may be added to current contributions to meet the 15% ceiling, but a deduction in excess of the 15% ceiling is not allowed.

Special rules apply if contributions in one taxable year are less than the 15% deductible limit but contributions in some succeeding taxable year exceed the 15% ceiling. A credit carryover allows part or all of the unused deduction to be used in the later year when contributions exceed the 15% limit, subject to certain restrictions. In the later year and in all subsequent years in which current contributions plus contribution carryovers exceed the 15% limit, the plan's total deduction is equal to the lesser of:

1. 25% of compensation for the later year, or
2. The excess of the combined 15% limits for the year and all prior years over the total deductions allowable for all prior years.

The purpose of the above deduction formula is to produce deductions over a period of years that average 15% of compensation.

When a company contribution is made after the time allowed, the company may claim a credit carryover in a later year.

Keep in mind that profit-sharing contributions must stay within the $30,000 ($45,475 in 1982)/25% limitations on annual additions to employee accounts. If these limits are exceeded, the plan could be disqualified and no deductions would be allowed.

Defined-benefit pension plans. Generally, the maximum deductible contribution is the amount necessary to fund current plan liabilities and amortize past service costs determined actuarially. This maximum deduction applies only if it allows a greater deduction than that determined under a level cost method or normal cost method detailed in the law. After 1982 a deduction may not be claimed for benefits which exceed those allowed under the $90,000/100% of average pay limit for defined-benefits plans. Anticipated cost-of-living increases may not be taken into account.

Defined-contribution pension plans. A company may deduct its contributions to a money-purchase plan (fixed contributions, regardless of profits) up to the limit for annual additions to an employee's account: 25% of compensation or $30,000 ($45,475 in 1982). If the plan exceeds the annual addition ceilings, the plan could be disqualified and no deduction allowed.

Deduction for multiple plans. If contributions are made to more than one profit-sharing plan, the total deduction is limited to 15% of the covered employee's compensation. If contributions are made to more than one pension plan, each plan is subject to the deduction rules based on funding costs (see above).

If employees are covered by both a defined-benefit pension plan and a profit-sharing plan, the deduction for each plan is limited as discussed above and, in addition, there is an overall limitation. The total deduction may not exceed 25% of employees' compensation; any excess is deductible in subsequent years subject to the 25% limitation.

When deductions are claimed

Your company claims a deduction in the year the contribution is made. However, the company may deduct a contribution made within the period ending on the due date for filing the return for that taxable year (including extensions of time).

EXAMPLES—

1. Your corporation reports on a calendar year basis. For 1982 it may deduct a contribution made any time on or before March 15, 1983—the date a calendar-year corporation must file its return.
2. Your corporation receives a two-month extension until May 15, 1983. A payment made on or before May 15, 1983, is deductible on the 1982 tax return.
3. Your corporation has a fiscal year ending May 31, 1982. Its return is due August 15, 1982. It may make a deductible contribution for the 1982 fiscal year on or before August 15, 1982.

Important: In order to claim a deduction you must set up the trust for the plan before the close of the taxable year in which the plan is to be effective.

When benefits are paid

Benefits must generally begin to be paid no later than 60 days after the close of the plan year in which the last of these events occurs:

1. The employee reaches age 65 or earlier normal retirement age.
2. The employee completes ten years of plan participation.
3. The employee terminates employment.

An employee may elect to delay the receipt of benefits. Similarly, a plan may allow for early retirement if certain service requirements are met. If a plan permits a currently employed person who has satisfied a service requirement to elect an early-retirement benefit, it must allow a past employee the same right to receive benefit payments on an actuarily reduced basis. For example, if the plan provides a monthly benefit of $100 at age 55 for those currently employed and with 30 years of service, a terminated employee who had completed 30 years of service when he or she quit at age 50 could receive a monthly benefit beginning at age 55. The benefit would be actuarily reduced.

If the plan provides that benefits will be paid as an annuity and if the employee is married, the annuity will automatically be a joint and survivor annuity unless the employee elects otherwise. A written election is made prior to the starting date of the annuity.

For plan years after December 31, 1983, there will be a new mandatory distribution rule. Company plans will have to require that benefits begin in the year the employee reaches age 70½, or if later, the year of retirement. Distributions to key employees must begin at age 70½, whether or not they are retired.

If an employee dies before his entire interest is paid, or a surviving spouse receiving payments dies before the entire interest is received, the balance will generally have to be distributed to the beneficiaries within five years. There is an exception if the employee had started to receive benefits over a period not exceeding the joint lives of the employee and his or her spouse.

How benefits from qualified company plans are taxed

The method of payment determines how benefits are taxed. Special tax benefits are given to a lump-sum distribution from a qualified plan. You may apply the ten-year averaging method for the entire distribution. Alternatively, you may avoid immediate taxation by making a tax-free rollover of all or part of your lump-sum distribution to another qualified plan or individual retirement account. If you receive your benefits as an annuity, you are taxed at ordinary income rates on the part of the payment attributable to employer contributions.

To qualify a lump-sum distribution for ten-year averaging, you must receive all that is due you under the plan. A distribution of part of your account is not a lump-sum distribution. The payment or payments must be made within one of your taxable years (usually a calendar year). The distribution must be made because you are either separated from service, reached the age of 59½, or died. When you reach age 59½, you may receive a lump sum qualifying for special tax treatment even if you continue to work. Finally, you must be in the plan for at least five years.

If you die before collecting from the plan, your beneficiary does not have to meet the five-year test. He or she may elect ten-year averaging even if you die before age 59½.

The ten-year averaging rule is discussed in greater detail in Chapter 8, and rollovers are discussed in Chapter 9.

Obtaining plan approval

Obtaining approval from the IRS is not necessary to qualify the plan for tax benefits, but it is advisable because of the technical tests that a plan must meet. Failure to comply will disqualify the plan and bar all tax benefits.

Use of model or prototype plans offered by an institution may avoid having to obtain a determination letter.

For advance approval, a copy of the plan must be submitted to the IRS, along with Forms 5001 and 5002.

What happens to benefits when an employee terminates employment?

Benefits that are fully vested belong to an employee even if he or she quits or is fired. The plan can specify whether to pay the benefits immediately in a lump sum or freeze the benefits until the employee reaches retirement age.

A plan can require a payout of benefits if their present value is less than $1750. This is called an involuntary cash-out. If the employee resumes employment, he can elect to put the sum back into the plan if the original cash-out was less than the present value of his accrued benefits.

Benefits paid out upon employment termination may be

rolled over to an IRA or a qualified plan of a new employer if certain conditions are met.

Benefits which do not vest to an employee are forfeited if the employee quits. The benefits remain in the plan. In pension plans, forfeitures are used to reduce employer contributions. Profit-sharing plans may also use forfeitures to reduce employer contributions, but in practice many profit-sharing plans allocate forfeitures to the accounts of the remaining employees. In a Subchapter S corporation plan, forfeited benefits may not be used to benefit stockholder-employees.

If an employee dies before retirement, the forfeiture of vested benefits attributable to company contributions may be allowed. However, forfeiture in this case is not allowed if the employee chose to continue working past the normal retirement age when he or she could have selected a joint and survivor annuity.

An employee does not forfeit vested benefits by leaving to work for a competitor.

An employee's own contributions are immediately vested. Therefore they are not subject to forfeiture under any circumstances. However, in a plan where employee contributions are required along with employer contributions, forfeiture of employer contributions may have this result: if an employee's benefit attributable to employer's contributions is less than 50% vested, that benefit is forfeitable if the employee withdraws part or all of his contributions. Under a buy-back rule, an employee can fully restore forfeited benefits if withdrawn contributions, plus interest, are returned to the plan.

Contributions to Subchapter S corporate plans

Retirement benefits for shareholder-employees of Subchapter S corporations are limited. Shareholder-employees are officers or employees owning more than 5% of the stock; under the 5% rule, stock owned by a spouse, child, parent, or grandparent is considered owned by the employee.

Benefits for Subchapter S shareholder-employees are limited similarly to benefits under self-employed Keogh plans. Whether the Subchapter S corporation adopts a defined-contribution pension plan or a defined-benefit pension plan, shareholder-employees must report as taxable pay any contribution in excess of the lesser of 15% of compensation or $15,000. In a defined-contribution plan, the corporation may nevertheless make deductible contributions up to the regular $30,000 ($45,475 in 1982)/25% limit for defined-contribution plans without disqualifying the plan. However, excess contributions above the $15,000/15% level could adversely affect the plan's qualified status if the total contribution discriminates in favor of shareholder-employees. If a shareholder-employee must report excess contributions as taxable pay under the $15,000/15% rule, the taxable amount may be recovered tax free when benefits are later received.

Beginning after December 31, 1983, Subchapter S shareholders will no longer be taxed on contributions in excess of the $15,000/15% level.

If the Subchapter S corporation's plan is a profit-sharing or stock-bonus plan, it must, to retain its qualified status, specifically provide that any forfeitures attributable to deductible contributions may not be allocated to the account of any shareholder-employee for that taxable year; they may be used to reduce company contributions or may be allocated to employees who are not shareholder-employees. This rule will no longer apply starting in 1984.

If a Subchapter S plan is a defined-benefit pension plan, special contribution rules govern benefit accruals. These are the same rules that apply to defined-benefit plans of the self-employed, explained in Chapter 4.

Substantial loans from company plans may be taxed

Your company plan may permit loans to employees, but there are limits on the amount that may be borrowed tax free. Loans made after August 13, 1982 may be taxed as a distribution under the following rules: A loan which is payable within five years is treated as a distribution only to the extent that it exceeds (when added to other outstanding loans from the plan) the lower of $50,000 or one-half of the present value of the employee's nonforfeitable plan benefit, but not less than $10,000. Thus employees may borrow at least $10,000 with no tax consequences, as long as the loan is repayable within five years. Further, if the loan is used to buy, construct, or rehabilitate a principal residence of the employee or an employee's relative, a loan within the $50,000/$10,000 limitation is tax free even if it is not repaid within five years.

In all other cases, loans which are not payable within five years are treated as a distribution from the plan.

The rules do not affect loans which were outstanding on August 13, 1982 if they are extended or renegotiated after that date as long as they are repaid before August 14, 1983. If they are not repaid by this date, they are treated as new loans on the date of renewal or renegotiation and are subject to the above limitations.

Reporting requirements

The law imposes reporting requirements to different sources: to employees, to the IRS, to the Department of Labor, and in some instances to the Pension Benefit Guaranty Corporation (PBGC). Some reports are required annually; others for specified events.

Stiff penalities are imposed on the employer or plan administrator for failure to comply with reporting requirements.

Chapter 6

SIMPLIFIED EMPLOYEE PENSION
PLANS (SEPs)

WHETHER you are a sole proprietor, partner, or the owner of a closely held corporation, you may want to provide yourself and your employees with pension benefits without the complicated paperwork and administrative costs entailed in corporate or Keogh plans. As an employer you can set up a pension plan without creating a trust; your company merely prepares checks which are mailed to each employee's individual retirement account (IRA) or annuity. The plan is called a Simplified Employee Pension Plan, or SEP.

Under an SEP, your company may make deductible contributions to an IRA account set up by each employee. The employee reports the contribution as income but claims an offsetting deduction.

To establish an SEP, an employer need take only the following steps:

1. Sign Form 5305–SEP and give a copy of it to each employee (the form is not filed with the IRS).
2. Make a "written allocation formula," that is, set the percentage of salary used for making contributions for all covered employees.

A decision to set up an SEP should be based on a review of the after-tax cost of providing contributions and the advantages and disadvantages of the SEP compared with other pension plan alternatives.

How SEPs compare with other plans

An SEP is a pension alternative for either an incorporated or an unincorporated business. A corporation can have either a qualified pension or profit-sharing or other similar plan and/or an SEP; an unincorporated business can have a Keogh plan and/or an SEP. However, an employer who has a defined-benefit plan for a self-employed person or a shareholder-employee may not also have an SEP.

The chief advantage of an SEP over other alternatives is simplicity. No formal plans or trusts are required. No special plan approval is necessary. All that is required is the written allocation formula and completion of Form 5305–SEP which is a half-page form filled out by the employer. The allocation formula is not part of the form; only the company's name, plan participation requirements, and employer's signature are needed. The form is considered properly executed when all eligible employees have set up IRAs and copies of the completed form have been given to all employees. The form is not sent to the IRS.

Further, annual reporting is greatly simplified. Thus beyond contribution costs, the cost of maintaining an SEP is virtually minimal.

While SEPs offer an employer the opportunity to set up a pension plan for a minimal expense and with greatly simplified reporting requirements, there are disadvantages. Lump-sum distributions from SEP–IRAs do not qualify for ten-year averaging. All distributions are fully taxable as ordinary income.

Another problem exists for employers who chose an SEP. The participation rule requires that all employees (with the exception of those whose earnings are $200 or less per year, certain union employees, and nonresident aliens) who are at least 25 years old and have performed service during at least three of the immediately preceding five calendar years must have contributions made to their accounts if the employer chooses to make any contributions for the year. Even the accounts of employees who have died or left the employer during the year for whatever reason must receive a contribution. For example, an employee who is otherwise eligible to participate quits in July. When contributions are made in December, the employee must receive his allocable share. Failure to give the employee his share could disqualify the entire plan. If the employee did not establish an SEP–IRA or closed it prior to the time contributions are made, the employer must set up an IRA on the employee's behalf. The employer must send notice of the contribution in person or to the last known address of such employee. Additionally, the employer must keep a record of the payments and the institution where the employee's account is maintained.

The SEP participation rules differ from corporate and Keogh plans which focus on years of completed service. In a corporate plan an employee who is 25 years old or who has completed one year of service must be covered. (A three-year rule may apply in certain plans.) A year of service is defined as at least 1000 hours in a 12-month period. Thus certain part-time employees can be excluded. Similarly, Keogh plans can exclude part-time employees because only those who have completed three years of service need be covered. In an SEP, except for those earning below $200 all employees, including part-timers who have worked in three consecutive years, must be covered.

While the $15,000/15% of earnings limitation on deductible contributions is currently the same for Keogh plans and SEPs, a Keogh plan offers this advantage over an SEP: voluntary contributions may be made up to certain limits. While not deductible, the income earned on such contributions may accumulate tax free. After 1983 there is no ceiling on voluntary contributions to Keoghs.

Limits on SEP contributions

The maximum contribution in 1982 and 1983 is 15% of compensation (exclusive of SEP contributions) or $15,000, whichever is less. Contributions must be made under a written allocation formula which is merely a percentage for figuring contributions. Contributions must bear a uniform relationship to the total compensation (not in excess of $200,000) of each employee. For example, an allocation formula calling for contributions of 10% of compensation would be acceptable. A contribution rate which decreases as compensation increases is considered uniform. To illustrate, an allocation formula may call for a contribution based on 7.5% of an employee's first $10,000 of compensation and 5% of all compensation over $10,000. After 1983 the maximum contribution increases to the lesser of 25% of compensation or $30,000, the same limitation applied to all defined-contribution plans.

The allocation formula does not commit an employer to

making contributions. Contributions remain discretionary and can be made one year and not another, without regard to profits or any other criteria. Thus if you have a good year you may make contributions, but are not forced to do so if you have a bad year.

Contributions may not discriminate in favor of employees who are officers, shareholders who owned more than 10% of the value of the employer's stock, self-employed individuals, or highly compensated employees. Contributions are deemed discriminatory unless they bear a uniform relationship to the total compensation of each employee with an SEP. The percentage for figuring the contribution must generally be the same. If at least $100,000 (but not more than $200,000) of compensation is taken into account, contributions on behalf of all employees must be at least 7.5%. For example, if the maximum contribution of $15,000 is made to the SEP of an employee whose total compensation is $220,000, at least 7.5% must be used as a base for figuring contributions for other employees because $15,000 is 7.5% of $200,000 (only the first $200,000 of compensation is taken into account). Compensation means wages, salaries, professional fees, and other amounts received for services actually rendered but does not include amounts excludable from gross income (e.g., foreign earned income).

An employer makes contributions to an employee's individual retirement account or individual retirement annuity. The model SEP provides that the employer pay contributions to each employee's IRA trustee, custodian, or insurance company (in the case of an annuity contract). The employee must set up the SEP with a bank, insurance company, or other qualified institution; the employer merely pays the contribution.

An employer is allowed to count its payment of Social Security taxes (FICA) on behalf of each employee as an employer contribution. This reduces the employer's cost. The treatment of FICA as an employer contribution is called integration. Integration may result in a lower effective rate of contribution for lower paid employees than for higher paid employees but this discrepancy is not considered discriminatory. The IRS has not yet provided a vehicle for implementing integration with FICA. The model SEP, Form 5305–SEP, may *not* be used for plans integrated with or offset by employer FICA payments; the model may only be used for nonintegrated plans. Also, if the plan is integrated with Social Security, the maximum contribution, $15,000 for shareholder-employees and owner-employees, must be reduced by FICA and self-employment taxes. Thus the maximum contribution for a shareholder-employee in an integrated plan in 1982 is $12,849; the maximum contribution for an owner-employee in an integrated plan in 1982 is $11,971.

No FICA or FUTA taxes need be withheld on employer contributions.

If your employer has an SEP

From an employee's perspective, an SEP is just like an IRA. The investment vehicle, an account with a bank or other financial institution or an annuity from an insurance company, may be left to the employee's discretion. Employees may choose different investment vehicles or different companies offering the same type of investments. Employers may wish to encourage the use of the same bank for IRA accounts by all employees for the sake of convenience in checking on the establishment of accounts by all eligible employees and in making contributions, but this cannot be required. The establishment of an IRA may be a condition of employment.

Employees can use existing IRAs provided the bank or other trustee or custodian amends the terms of the account to accept contributions up to $15,000, since regular IRA sponsors may not accept contributions in excess of $2000 other than rollovers.

An employer's contribution under an SEP has no effect on an employee's personal IRA contribution. Thus regardless of the amount the employer contributes, the employee can contribute up to $2000 annually to an IRA. The maximum total deduction on the employee's return is $17,000 ($15,000 for the SEP and $2000 for the IRA). An employee aged 70½ can claim a deduction for an SEP contribution even though a contribution to an IRA is barred.

The amount of the employer's contribution is included in the gross income figure reported on the employee's Form W-2. However, the form also separately identifies the contribution so the employee may claim the amount as an offsetting deduction.

If the employer makes a contribution after the close of the calendar year, an amended W-2 must be issued to the employee.

All employee benefits are 100% vested, and there can be no prohibitions against withdrawals.

How SEP benefits are taxed

The employee with an SEP is subject to the same income tax treatment imposed on regular IRAs. SEP distributions are taxed at ordinary income rates and do not qualify for special tax treatment.

SEPs may be rolled over to other IRA investment vehicles. As with regular IRAs no more than one rollover may be made within the year, but direct transfers between trustees do not constitute rollovers.

SEPs are subject to the same penalties imposed on regular IRAs. Thus the funds must generally remain in the account until age 59½; premature withdrawals are costly.

Reporting rules

Congress created the SEP to provide a pension vehicle with minimal reporting requirements. The employer's only reporting requirement is to show the contribution on the employee's Form W-2. This must be done by January 31 of the year following the year of contribution, or 30 days after the contribution was made, whichever is later. Thus a 1982 contribution made in November is reported on the employee's W-2 which is supplied by the end of January. If a 1982 contribution is made on February 1, 1983, an amended W-2 should be supplied by March 1, 1983.

Chapter 7

DEFERRED PAY PLANS FOR INCREASED RETIREMENT BENEFITS

IF your company has a profit-sharing or stock bonus plan, it may give you the opportunity to shelter additional pay from tax. The tax law permits the company to add a cash or deferred-pay arrangement, also called a salary-reduction plan, to its existing plan. The cash or deferred-pay plan was sanctioned by a law change in 1978 but was not widely adopted until the IRS released recently proposed regulations on how the plan was to operate.

The cash or deferred-pay plan works in one of two ways:

1. Your employer contributes an amount for your benefit to a trust account. You are not taxed on your employer's contribution.
2. You agree to take a salary reduction or to forgo a salary increase. An amount equal to the pay reduction is placed in a trust account for your benefit. The reduction is treated as your employer's contribution.

Income earned on the trust account accumulates tax free until it is withdrawn. At withdrawal, the tax on the proceeds may be computed by use of the ten-year averaging method. This method is explained in detail in Chapter 8.

There are restrictions on when benefits can be withdrawn. You may not withdraw funds until you reach age 59½, retire, are separated from service (resign or have been discharged), become disabled, or show financial hardship. Each plan may define financial hardship.

Should you take a salary reduction?

Taking a pay reduction may be an ideal way to defer income, benefit from a tax-free buildup of income, and take advantage of ten-year averaging at distribution. However, if your salary is under the base for Social Security taxes, a reduction in salary may affect your future Social Security benefits.

EXAMPLE—

You earn $30,000 and agree to defer 10% of your pay by taking a salary reduction. $3000 is put into a trust and your taxable pay reported on your Form W-2 for the year is $27,000, which you report on your tax return. No Social Security or other payroll taxes are withheld on the $3000 put into the plan, but as a result fewer wages are credited to your Social Security record. Income earned on the $3000 deposit is not taxed. When you withdraw your total account, you may be able to pay tax on the distribution using ten-year averaging.

Some authorities contend that any possible decrease in Social Security coverage would be more than offset by increases in additional retirement benefits from the cash or deferred-pay plan. Clearly, for those who earn more than the Social Security tax base, agreeing to a salary reduction would not affect Social Security benefits.

Participating in a deferred-pay or salary-reduction plan does not prevent you from also contributing to an IRA account. However, if your investment dollars are limited and you must choose between setting up your own IRA or contributing to a salary-reduction plan, consider the relative merits of each plan.

With an IRA, you must take the initiative to seek out an investment, such as a bank CD or an annuity. Further, you must meet your contribution obligation yourself. With a salary reduction plan, you have to do nothing more than consent. The plan is set up and administered by your company plan's trustees. Contributions are automatic; they are withheld from your pay and transferred to the plan.

The maximum salary reduction contribution is not a fixed dollar amount but rather a percentage of compensation. Salary reductions are treated as employer contributions. If total company retirement plan contributions are limited to 15% of compensation and the company contributes 10% to a profit-sharing plan, the limitation on an employee's salary reduction would be 5%. If the company plans to match employee contributions, the salary reduction limitation would be 2½%. This means that workers with greater earnings will be able to contribute more to the plan than workers with smaller earnings. Assume a plan permits salary reduction up to 5% of compensation. For workers earning less than $40,000, contributions would be below the amount that could be put into an IRA; for those earning above $40,000, contributions to a salary-reduction plan would outstrip IRA contributions. For example, an executive earning $60,000 could contribute $2000 to an IRA. That same executive could have his or her salary reduced by 5% or $3000 and have that money contributed to the company's plan.

The current tax saving for an equal amount of money put into an IRA or into a salary-reduction plan is the same. However, a salary-reduction plan produces this tax benefit: no FICA taxes are withheld on the amount you contribute. This becomes important for those below the maximum FICA contribution base. For example, in 1982 you earn $25,000 and agree to put 5%, or $1250, of your pay in the plan. FICA is withheld on only $23,750. Since the FICA rate for 1982 is 6.7%, a savings of $84 results. Not only does the employee save on FICA, but the employer also saves. The employer does not have to contribute to FICA or FUTA on the amount of the salary reduction. This works out to an employer savings of about 10¢ on every $1 of salary reduction.

Cash or deferred-pay plan may not discriminate

For a plan to qualify, it may not discriminate in favor of highly compensated employees. To judge whether there is discrimination, employees are grouped as follows: higher paid one-third and lower paid two-thirds. One of two percentage tests must be satisfied: (1) the average percentage of pay contributed by the higher paid one-third group is not more than 1½ times the average percent of pay contributed by the lower paid two-thirds, or (2) the average percentage contribution for the top one-third group is no more than 3% greater than the average percentage contribution for the lower two-thirds. The average percentage contribution for the top one-third must also be no more than 2½ times the average percentage for the lower two-thirds. Thus if the lower paid group deferred an average 2% of their pay, the upper one-third group could average as much as 5% deferral without creating a discrimination problem.

For the employer, the discrimination issue presents a real problem. While the plan is offered to all employees, there is no way to know in advance how many and to what extent employees will take up the pay-reduction option. Salary reductions cannot be mandatory. What happens if an employer offers the plan but only highly paid employees decide to defer pay? The plan is disqualified and contributions are currently taxed, but plan contributions are probably still locked into the plan until age 59½. Generally, employers need not fear a discrimination problem. Where the plan has been offered, employee acceptance has been enthusiastic. When one large company offered the plan, 85% of its employees chose to participate.

How benefits are taxed. All IRA distributions, whether paid in a lump sum or periodic installments, are subject to the same tax treatment: distributions are added to your other income and taxed at ordinary income tax rates. However, distributions from salary-reduction plans may receive special tax treatment. If the distribution is paid out in a lump sum, it may qualify for special ten-year averaging. This method results in considerably lower tax on the distribution than if ordinary income tax rates applied.

Restrictions. IRA and salary-reduction plans are subject to similar restrictions in that the funds may not generally be touched until age 59½, unless you are disabled. Withdrawing money sooner incurs tax penalties. However, the salary-reduction plan allows withdrawals without a penalty prior to age 59½ if you leave the company or in the case of substantial financial hardship. Exactly what substantial financial hardship means has yet to be determined. The IRS has said only that it must be "immediate and heavy." Each plan must set up a board or committee to review claimed hardships on a case-by-case basis, according to uniform and nondiscriminatory standards set forth in the plan. It has been suggested that the hardship test may be liberally construed. For example, inability to get a home mortgage at a reasonable rate may be a sufficient hardship to warrant a penalty-free distribution. There is, of course, the question of privacy and how much financial and personal disclosure the plan's committee can legally require. A statement by an employee claiming hardship may be all that is required.

Salary-reduction plans for employees of tax-exempt groups and schools

If you are employed by a tax-exempt religious, charitable, or educational organization, or if you are on the civilian staff or faculty of the Uniformed Services University of the Health Sciences (Department of Defense), you may be able to purchase a tax-deferred retirement annuity, generally through a salary reduction which pays for the contract. Salary reductions are treated as employer contributions. Contributions may be invested in mutual fund shares as well as in annuity contracts.

The amount of the salary reduction is not taxable if it comes within these rules: the tax-sheltered contribution is generally 20% of your pay multiplied by the number of years of service with your employer, less salary reductions or employer contributions to the annuity which were tax free in prior taxable years. However, a contribution may be taxable to the extent it exceeds the lesser of 25% of compensation, or the defined-contribution dollar limit which is $45,475 in 1982 and $30,000 after 1982.

EXAMPLE—

Your salary is $20,000 and your contribution computed under the 20% rule is $4000. Assuming that this is your first year of service, you are not taxed on the $4000 contribution as it comes within the 20% limit: 20% of $20,000 ($20,000 × 1 year service) or $4000. It also comes within the 25% contribution limit: 25% of $20,000, or $5000.

Employees of schools, hospitals, and home health services may specially elect to make tax-free contributions greater than those allowed under the 25% of compensation ceiling but which fall within the general 20% of pay exclusion. Such employees may elect to exclude from pay the lowest of: (1) the general 20% of pay/years of service exclusion discussed earlier; (2) 25% of pay plus $4000; or (3) $15,000. Once this election is made for any year, the election is irrevocable and will apply to all future years.

Employees of schools, hospitals, and home health agencies may make an irrevocable election to disregard the general 20% of pay test. If the election is made, the annual tax-free contribution equals the contribution limit for defined-contribution plans which is the lesser of 25% of pay, or the dollar limit of $45,475 in 1982 or $30,000 after 1982.

The above contribution rules have been stated in general terms and other elections may be available, as explained in temporary Treasury regulations. You should ask your employer or the issuer of the contract to compute the maximum tax-free contribution.

Church employees. For duly ordained ministers and church lay employees with adjusted gross income of $17,000 or less (without regard to their spouse's income), tax-free contributions may be made up to the lesser of $3000 or taxable compensation, even if this exceeds the amount otherwise allowable under the general 20% of pay/years of service test. Further, such church employees may make an election which allows contributions to be made in excess of the defined-contribution limitation. If the election is made, contributions of up to $10,000 may be made for any one year, subject to a lifetime limitation of $40,000. Such contributions are tax free if they are within the 20% of pay exclusion.

How annuity distributions are taxed. If benefits are paid as an annuity, each installment is fully taxable if all of the contributions were tax free under the above rules. If excess contributions were taxable, you may recover this amount tax free. If benefits are in the form of a lump-sum distribution, a rollover may be made to an IRA account. If you do not make a rollover, the lump sum is taxed as ordinary income; the special ten-year averaging method allowed for lump-sum distributions from qualified company plans is not available.

Chapter 8
RETIREMENT BENEFIT OPTIONS

BEFORE you reach retirement age, you should consider how and when you will take your retirement benefits. Project how much you will be entitled to receive from your plan upon retirement. If you are covered by a company plan, remember that your benefits must be "vested" in order for you to receive them. Will you take distributions in a lump sum or on an annuity basis? Your choice of payment method will affect your tax. For example, lump-sum distributions receive more favorable tax treatment than annuities.

Are your employee benefits vested?

If you are covered by a company plan, you are not assured of a payout upon retirement unless you have vested benefits. If you retire or leave the company before the number of years specified in the company's vesting schedule, you will not receive all the benefits which have accrued on your behalf.

As an employee, your benefits from your own contributions are always 100% vested. The law provides minimum vesting requirements for benefits from employer contributions. Your company must adopt a vesting schedule which is at least as beneficial as *one* of the following:

1. Full vesting after ten years. When you have completed ten years of service, your benefits from employer contributions are 100% vested. If you leave the company before completing ten years of service, you are not entitled to any benefits.

2. Gradual vesting. After five years of service, 25% of your accrued benefits from employer contributions become nonforfeitable. For each of the next five years vested benefits increase

106

by 5%, so that after ten years your benefits are 50% vested. For each of the next five years vesting increases by 10%, so that after 15 years your benefits are 100% vested.

3. Rule of 45 vesting. Your benefits are 50% vested when your age plus years of service total at least 45, or after ten years of service, whichever occurs first. Once your benefits are 50% vested, 10% is vested for each additional year of service.

4. Class-year plans. Your company may vest each year's contribution separately. In such plans your benefits from employer contributions must be 100% vested no later than the end of the fifth plan year after the year of the contribution.

5. Special vesting for top-heavy plans. If you are covered by a plan that is determined to be top heavy, special vesting rules apply after 1983. These rules are discussed in Chapter 5.

Keep in mind that these are minimum vesting requirements. Your company may allow more rapid vesting. Ask the administrator of your company plan to give you a copy of the plan description which includes the vesting schedule.

Generally, you will be credited with a year of service if you have worked 1000 hours in a consecutive 12-month period. The company does not have to include years of service before age 22 unless it uses the rule of 45 to determine vesting. If, before you had any vested benefits, you had a "break in service" (i.e., you worked no more than 500 hours within a 12-month period), your company does not have to count your employment before the break if it is less than the period of the break itself.

In some cases a plan may have different years of service requirements: one for figuring accrued benefits and another for vesting purposes. For example, years of service after age 22 are counted for purposes of vesting, although the plan may not start providing benefits until age 25. (See Chapter 5 for coverage requirements.) Your plan administrator can tell you if your accrued and vested benefits differ.

When to take retirement benefits

When you should take retirement benefits is a decision governed in part by the terms of your plan and in part by personal wishes and needs. Here are the earliest and latest dates you may receive benefits without tax penalty or loss of tax advantages.

Qualified pension, profit-sharing, or stock-bonus plans. The earliest date for receiving retirement benefits is the date set forth in the plan as retirement age, typically age 65. Some plans provide an early retirement date at which time a participant can receive a payout, although benefits will be permanently reduced. Most plans provide for the payment of benefits in case of disability.

You must begin to receive benefits no later than 60 days after the taxable year in which the latest of these events occurs: you

1. Reach normal retirement age as set forth in the plan;
2. Terminate employment; or
3. Complete ten years of participation in the plan.

Beginning in 1984 your entire interest must be distributed to you (1) no later than the taxable year in which you reach age 70½, or in the year of retirement, whichever is later, or (2) over your life (or over the lives of you and your spouse); or over a period not extending beyond your life expectancy (or the life expectancy of you and your spouse) as long as distributions begin by age 70½, or the year of retirement, whichever is later. Beginning in 1984 owners and certain key employees must begin to take retirement benefits in the year they reach age 70½, even if they do not retire.

Employers covered by Keogh plans. A self-employed individual may not receive benefits before he or she reaches age 59½ unless totally disabled. You are considered disabled if you cannot hold a job because of an illness that can be expected to be of long and indefinite duration or to result in death. A Keogh plan must provide that the restriction of payments before age 59½, except for disability (or death), applies even if the plan is terminated. These restrictions do not apply to voluntary (nondeductible) contributions which may be withdrawn at any time.

Your entire interest must be paid to you:

1. No later than the taxable year in which you are age 70½;
   or
2. Over your life, or over the lives of you and your spouse, or

over a period not extending beyond your life expectancy or the life expectancy of you and your spouse, provided that the distributions begin no later than the taxable year in which you are age 70½.

If you die before retirement, your interest as an owner-employee must be:

1. Paid within five years after your death (or that of your surviving spouse) to your beneficiaries; or
2. Within the same five-year time limit used to purchase an immediate annuity payable over the beneficiary's life, or for a period not longer than the beneficiary's life expectancy.

If you die after distributions have begun, the five-year restrictions do not apply, provided the distributions were geared to the joint life expectancy of you and your spouse.

Employees covered by Keogh plans. As an employee, you are subject to different rules. There is no minimum age at which benefits may begin. Benefits must begin, however, no later than 60 days after the taxable year in which the latest of these events occurs: (1) you reach normal retirement age as set forth in the plan; (2) you terminate employment; or (3) you complete ten years of participation in the plan.

Beginning in 1984 your entire interest must be distributed:

1. No later than the taxable year in which you are 70½, or the year in which you retire, whichever is later; or
2. Over your life, or over the lives of you and your spouse, or over a period not extending beyond your life expectancy or the life expectancy of you and your spouse, provided the distributions begin no later than the taxable year in which you are 70½ or the year in which you retire, whichever is later.

Individual retirement plans. Benefits may begin after age 59½. If you are disabled, there is no penalty if you take benefits before age 59½.

By age 70½ you must receive a lump-sum distribution or begin to receive a distribution figured to exhaust your account over the remainder of your life, or the joint life and last survivor expectancy of you and your spouse.

How to take retirement benefits

Whether you will receive benefits monthly, quarterly, or in a lump sum may be determined by your retirement plan. Some qualified plans will only pay benefits as an annuity while others will only make a lump-sum distribution. If you are given the option of how to take benefits, consider not only your personal and financial needs but the tax consequences of your choice. Lump-sum distributions receive favorable tax treatment; annuities do not.

When you receive a lump-sum distribution from a qualified plan, you face a choice: Should you opt to have the use of your money but pay tax now, or defer tax but do without the use of the money? Personal considerations may require that you take the money now and therefore pay tax now. However, if personal considerations do not dictate your decision, tax effects should be considered.

If you must pay tax now, you might qualify for special tax treatment called ten-year averaging. Tax under the ten-year averaging rule is figured separately and apart from tax on your other income and the portion of the distribution qualifying as capital gain (see below). The effect of the averaging method is to tax the ordinary-income portion of a lump-sum distribution as if it were received evenly over a ten-year period. This results in a substantially lower tax than if the distribution were included with your other income and taxed at regular income tax rates.

Ten-year averaging is computed on Form 4972 with the tax taken from the unmarried individuals' tax rate schedule (single), regardless of your marital or head-of-household status. The separate tax figured under the ten-year averaging rule is added to your regular tax. This means that you do not include the ordinary-income element in your income when you compute your regular tax. Use of ten-year averaging does not bar you from applying the regular averaging rules to your other income and capital gain.

Here are sample effective tax rates on various distributions:

Amount of distribution	Effective tax rate in:		
	1982	1983	1984
Under $20,000	6%	5.5%	5.5%
$25,000	8.1%	7.4%	7.2%
$30,000	9.6%	8.9%	8.5%
$40,000	12%	11.2%	10.6%
$50,000	13.5%	12.5%	11.9%
$75,000	15.9%	14.5%	13.9%
$100,000	17.2%	15.4%	14.7%

These are the rates you would pay, regardless of your income tax bracket for other income.

Compare these rates with the rate you would pay on distributions in the future. If you roll over the distribution to an IRA, you lose forever your right to ten-year averaging even if you take your IRA distribution in a lump sum. In the future you may be in a lower tax bracket than you are when you receive the distribution, but will it be lower than the effective tax rate under ten-year averaging?

How to treat lump-sum distributions from qualified retirement plans

A lump-sum distribution from a qualified plan is subject to special tax rules. If you participated in a plan before 1974, contributions made before 1974 may be taxable as long-term capital gain. Part of a lump-sum distribution may be ordinary income taxable under the special ten-year averaging rule. You may even elect to apply the ten-year averaging method to the entire distribution. Alternatively, you may avoid immediate taxation by making a tax-free rollover of all or part of your lump-sum distribution to another qualified plan or an IRA. Distributions from an IRA do not qualify for capital gain treatment or ten-year averaging.

To qualify as a lump-sum distribution, these tests must be met:

1. Payment must be from a qualified pension or profit-sharing plan. A qualified plan is one approved by the IRS. A Civil Service retirement system that has a trust fund may be treated as a

qualified plan. Ask your retirement plan administrator whether your plan is qualified.

2. You must receive all that is due you under the plan. A distribution of only part of your account is not a lump-sum distribution. If your employer's plan uses more than one trust, you must receive a distribution of all that is due you from each trust.

3. The payment or payments must be made within one of your taxable years (usually a calendar year). For example, you retired on October 31, 1982, and start receiving monthly annuity payments under your company's plan on November 1, 1982. On February 3, 1983, you take the balance to your credit in lieu of any future annuity payments. The payments to you do not qualify as a lump sum; you did not receive them within one taxable year. However, if you had taken the balance of your account on or before December 31, 1982, all the payments would qualify.

4. If you are an employee, the distribution must be made because you are "separated from service" (discussed later), reach the age of 59½, or die. If you are self-employed, the lump-sum distribution from your Keogh plan must be made when you reach age 59½, become disabled, or die.

An employee who has reached age 59½ may receive a lump sum qualifying for special tax treatment even if he continues to work at his position. At one time the IRS said this was true only if the distribution was from a profit-sharing plan. However, the IRS agreed to apply the favorable rule to pension plans as well, provided the employee has reached both age 59½ and the normal retirement age as defined in the company plan.

Under some plans you receive an amount attributed to your last year of work after the year in which you were paid a lump sum. This payment does not affect special treatment of the lump sum. It is treated as the receipt of ordinary income because it was not paid in the same taxable year as the lump sum.

Effect of retroactive revocation of plan qualification on distribution. If a plan in which you participated loses its qualification, you may lose the tax benefits accorded to distributions from qualified plans.

EXAMPLE—

Woodson participated in a pension plan from 1966 until 1974 when the plan terminated and he received a net lump-sum distribution of $25,500 (excluding his contributions). In 1975 the IRS revoked the exempt status of the plan retroactively to 1973. Since the plan was nonqualified when Woodson's benefits were received, the IRS treated the entire distribution as ordinary income. Woodson argued that only $2643 in benefits, which were attributable to contributions made after the 1973 disqualification, were ordinary income; the rest of the distribution, relating to contributions made when the plan was qualified, should be taxed as capital gain.

The Tax Court, refusing to take an all-or-nothing approach, agreed. The tax character of the distribution is determined by the status of the trust at the time the contribution is made to it. Contributions made when the plan is qualified retain their qualified nature upon distribution.

On appeal, the Tax Court was reversed and the IRS position was upheld.

Capital gain and ordinary income portions are allocated. The company paying the lump-sum distribution has the responsibility of allocating the capital gain and ordinary-income portions on Form 1099R or other statement accompanying the distribution. Part of the lump-sum distribution representing the proportion of the number of years in which an employee was a member of a qualified plan before 1974 to the total number of years of participation is the capital gain portion. The balance attributed to the post-1973 participation period is taxable as ordinary income to which the ten-year averaging method may be applied.

More about ten-year averaging

You cannot use ten-year averaging unless you have been a participant in the plan for five or more years before the taxable year of the lump-sum distribution. If you receive lump-sum distributions from more than one qualified plan, you may elect the ten-year averaging method only once after you reach age 59½. Before age 59½ there is no limit to the number of times you may elect the ten-year averaging method. Filing Form 4972 acts as an election to use ten-year averaging.

If you are an employee, part of your lump-sum payment may be treated as long-term capital gain whether or not you elect ten-year averaging. That is, you will still treat part of your payment as capital gain although you participated in the plan for less than five years and therefore are not permitted to use the ten-year averaging method. Similarly, you may be barred from electing ten-year averaging because you already elected to use it once after you reached age 59½, although part of your payment may be capital gain.

If you are self-employed, part of your lump-sum distribution may be treated as capital gain only if you elect ten-year averaging. Thus you may not treat part of your payment as capital gain if you have not participated in the plan for more than five years.

If you are a beneficiary of a deceased employee, the five-year test does not apply. You may elect ten-year averaging whether or not the employee was a participant in the plan for more than five years. Further, you may elect ten-year averaging if the employee had not reached age 59½. However, if the employee was 59½ or older, you may elect ten-year averaging only once with respect to distributions you receive as his beneficiary. A lump-sum payment to you on account of the employee's death may qualify for capital gain and ten-year averaging treatment, although the employee received annuity payments before he died.

If you receive a lump-sum distribution but do not satisfy the five-year participation rule, you may not use ten-year averaging, but you may make a tax-free rollover to defer tax on the payment.

Election to treat capital gain as ordinary income. On Form 1099R your company lists the capital gain and ordinary-income elements of the distribution. You may want to elect to treat the entire lump-sum distribution from a qualified plan as ordinary income. In most situations the effective tax rate of ten-year averaging is less than the effective capital gain rate. This may be checked by computing the tax under both methods. The election is also advisable if you will be subject to alternative minimum tax on the capital gains portion. The election to treat the entire sum as ordinary income is made on Form 4972 simply by entering the entire distribution as ordinary income.

The election is irrevocable. Once you make it, all later lump-sum distributions from other qualified plans are treated as ordinary income. But you may not make this special election if after 1975 you received a lump-sum distribution and treated the pre-1974 element as long-term capital gain.

If you receive a lump-sum distribution as a beneficiary of a deceased employee, you may make the ordinary-income election; all later lump-sum distributions you receive as beneficiary of the same employee must also be treated as ordinary income. If you received a lump-sum distribution as beneficiary and treated the pre-1974 element as capital gain, you may not make this special election for any other lump sums you receive as beneficiary of the same employee.

The taxable portion of a lump-sum distribution does not include the employee's contributions to the plan and net unrealized appreciation on a distribution of securities of the employer.

EXAMPLE—

In 1982 an employee receives a lump-sum distribution of $65,000, including stock of his employer. The stock had a basis of $10,000 when put in the plan; it is valued at $25,000 when distributed, resulting in a net unrealized appreciation of $15,000. The employee did not contribute to the plan. The taxable portion of the distribution is $50,000 ($65,000 − $15,000). The $50,000 is then allocated between the capital gain and ordinary income portions.

Community property. Only the spouse who has earned the lump-sum distribution may apply the ten-year averaging method. Community-property laws are disregarded for purposes of computing this tax. If a couple filed separate returns and one spouse elects the ten-year averaging method, the other spouse is not taxable on the amount subject to the computation.

EXAMPLE—

A husband in a community-property state receives a lump-sum distribution of which the ordinary-income portion is

$10,000. He and his wife file separate returns. If the ten-year averaging computation is not elected, $5000, or one-half, is taxable in the husband's return and the other $5000 in his wife's return. However, if he elects the ten-year averaging method, only he reports the $10,000 on Form 4972.

Look-back rule for annuity contracts or receipt of more than one lump sum during a six-year period. The use of the ten-year averaging method is modified by a "look-back" provision which requires that the lump-sum distributions for the taxable year be aggregated with all post-1973 lump-sum distributions made during the five previous tax years. This increases the bracket at which the ordinary-income portion of the current year's lump-sum distribution is taxed. You do not aggregate lump sums paid before 1974 or post-1973 lump sums which were not subject to the ten-year averaging rule.

A look-back rule is also applied to the distribution of an annuity contract, although its total value is not taxable when distributed. The current actuarial value is included in the six-year aggregation computation to determine the taxable bracket of the ordinary income portion of a current lump-sum distribution. An example of computing tax when a distribution includes an annuity contract is in the instructions accompanying Form 4972.

Separation-from-service test for employees

Employees who have not reached the age of 59½ must be separated from service to be eligible for the favorable tax treatments accorded distributions. The separation-from-service test requires that you have retired, resigned, or have been discharged. If a plan is terminated but you continue working, distributions are not entitled to special lump-sum treatment if you have not reached age 59½. After you reach age 59½ the separation-from-service test need not be met. According to the IRS, if you receive a lump-sum distribution from a pension plan after age 59½, you also must have reached the normal retirement age as fixed in the company plan to qualify for special tax treatment.

The test generally prevents lump-sum treatment when a qualified plan is terminated following a reorganization or merger of a company. According to the IRS, an employee under age 59½ receiving a lump-sum distribution from the plan may not claim lump-sum treatment. This IRS position is a reversal of a prior policy under which lump-sum treatment was sometimes permitted. Under the current IRS position, payments following reorganization, liquidation, or merger are not considered lump-sum payments to employees remaining with the successor corporation. In one case, however, an appeals court held that a beneficial change in ownership and eventual liquidation of the employer corporation resulted in the employee's "separation from service."

Important: A lump sum paid on account of termination of a plan may be rolled over tax free to an individual retirement account.

Partnership plans. Lump-sum payments made on the termination of a plan when a partnership dissolves do not qualify for special lump-sum treatment when the employees continue to work for the successor partnership. Similarly, an employee of a partnership who becomes a partner and has to quit the firm's employee profit-sharing plan may not treat the payment as a lump sum. He or she is still serving the firm.

Lump-sum payments received by deceased employee's beneficiary

A beneficiary of a deceased employee may apply the special lump-sum rules to a payment received because of the employee's death. In addition, the $5000 death benefit exclusion may also be claimed. The $5000 exclusion for payments to beneficiaries of owners applies only for the case of owners who die after 1983. Any federal estate tax attributable to the distribution is deductible.

A beneficiary may elect to forgo the favorable income tax treatment for lump-sum benefits in order to reduce the estate tax on the distribution. Whether it is advisable to make this election is discussed in Chapter 11.

Payment received by a second beneficiary (after the death of the first beneficiary) is not entitled to lump-sum treatment or the death-benefit exclusion.

EXAMPLES—

1. Gunnison's father was covered by a company benefit plan. The father died, as did his widow, before benefits were fully paid out. Gunnison received a substantial lump sum and argued that he should be eligible to use lump-sum treatment because he collected benefits on account of his father's death. The IRS disagreed. The Tax Court and an appeals court sided with the IRS. Gunnison was entitled to the payment following his mother's death, not his father's death. The payout must arise solely on account of the death of the covered employee to qualify for special lump-sum treatment.

2. Robert's employer announced the termination of its pension plan. Before benefits were distributed, Robert died. His widow received a lump-sum distribution as his beneficiary. After subtracting the amount attributable to Robert's contributions, she excluded $5000 as a death benefit and treated the balance as a lump-sum distribution. The IRS claimed she received the distribution on the termination of the plan, not because of Robert's death. The Tax Court agreed. Distribution was made to her under the termination provisions, not the provisions for withdrawal due to separation from service or death. She could not take a death-benefit exclusion, and the distribution (less Robert's contributions) could not be treated as a lump-sum distribution.

Lump-sum distribution to more than one beneficiary. A lump-sum distribution to two or more individuals may qualify for capital gain treatment and the ten-year averaging method. The distribution is first treated as made to one recipient to determine whether it is a lump sum and what portion is taxable as capital gain. Each beneficiary may separately elect the ten-year averaging method for the ordinary-income portion, even if other beneficiaries do not.

Distribution to trust or estate. If a lump sum is paid to a trust or estate, the employee, or a personal representative if the employee is deceased, may elect to use the ten-year averaging method. This is true even though the ordinary-income portion is distributed to the beneficiaries in the year the lump sum was received. If the fiduciary makes the election, the ordinary income is taxable to the trust or estate even if a distribution is made to the beneficiary. However, the capital gain portion, if distributed to the beneficiaries in the year received by the trust or estate, is taxable as long-term capital gain to the beneficiaries, not to the trust. If the distribution is to the beneficiaries of a self-employed person, the beneficiaries may not treat the capital gain portion as capital gain unless the trust or estate also makes an election to use the ten-year averaging method.

Securities received as distribution

When your company plan distributes securities of the company, the amount reported as income depends on the value of the securities, the amount contributed by the company for the securities, and whether the distribution qualifies as a lump-sum payment.

Lump-sum payments. If the distribution is of appreciated securities and is part of a lump-sum distribution, the unrealized appreciation is not subject to tax at the time of distribution. Only the amount of the employer's contribution is subject to tax. Tax on the appreciation is delayed until the shares are later sold by you at a price exceeding cost basis. If, when distributed, the shares are valued at below the cost contribution of the employer, the fair market value of the shares is subject to tax. If you contributed to the purchase of the shares and their value is less than your contribution, you do not realize a loss deduction on the distribution. You realize a loss only when the stock is sold or becomes worthless at a later date. If a plan distributes worthless stock, you may deduct your contributions to the stock as an ordinary loss if you itemize deductions.

EXAMPLES—

1. Shares valued below your cost contribution. You contributed $500 and your employer contributed $300 to buy ten shares of company stock having a fair market value of $80 per share, or a total of $800. You do not realize income on the distribution, and you do not have a deductible loss for the difference between your cost contribution and the lower fair market value. Your contribution to the stock is its basis. This is $50 per share. If you sell the stock for $40 per share, you have a capital loss of $10 per share. However, if you sell the stock for $60 per share, you have gain of $10 per share.

2. Appreciated shares. You receive ten shares of company stock to which only the employer contributed toward their purchase. Your employer's cost was $50 a share. At the time of distribution the shares are valued at $80 a share. Your employer's contribution of $50 a share, or $500, is included as part of your taxable distribution. The appreciation of $300 is not included. The cost basis of the shares in your hands is $500 (the amount currently taxable to you). The holding period of the stock starts at the date of distribution. However, if you sell the shares for any amount exceeding $500 and up to $800, your profit is long-term gain even if the sale is within one year of the date of the distribution. If you sell for more than $800, the gain exceeding the original unrealized appreciation of $300 is subject to long-term capital gain treatment only if the sale is long term from the date of distribution. Thus if within a month of the distribution you sold the shares for $900, $300 would be long-term gain; $100 would be short-term gain.

Other than lump-sum payments. If you receive appreciated securities in a distribution that does not meet the lump-sum tests, you report as ordinary income the amount of the employer's contribution to the purchase of the shares and the appreciation allocated to his cost contribution. You do not report the amount of appreciation allocated to your contribution.

EXAMPLE—

A qualified plan distributes ten shares of company stock with an average cost of $100, of which the employee contributed $60 and the employer $40. At the date of distribution the stock had a fair market value of $180. The portion of the unrealized appreciation attributable to the employee's contribution is $48 (60% of $80); the employer's is $32 (40% of $80). The employee reports $72 as income; the employer's cost is $40 and his or her share of appreciation is $32. The basis of each share is $132, which includes employee contribution of $60 and the $72 reported as taxable income. Net unrealized appreciation and cost contributions must be supplied by the company distributing the stock.

How annuity payments are taxed

Retirement benefits paid as annuities are generally taxed in the same manner as commercial annuities. That is, part of the annuity payment is treated as a nontaxable return of your cost (premiums or other amounts as explained below); part is taxable income earned on your investment. But if your pension was completely financed by your employer and you did not include as income your employer's premium contributions, you report all periodic payments you receive as ordinary income. You have no cost investment in the annuity contract.

Figuring your cost factor. Cost includes the following items:

1. Premiums paid by you or by withholdings from your pay.
2. Payments made by your employer and reported as additional pay. Premiums paid by an employer in a nonapproved plan for your benefit give you immediate income if you have nonforfeitable rights to the policy.
3. Premiums paid by your employer which, if the amounts had been paid to you directly, would have been tax free to you because you were working abroad.
4. Pre-1939 contributions by a city or state to its employees' pension fund. (Before 1939 salary payments to state and city employees were tax free for federal income tax purposes.)
5. If you are a beneficiary collecting because of the death of an employee, cost may include all or part of the death-benefit exclusion up to $5000.

Three-year recovery of cost

If within three years of the first payment, payments under the contract will equal or exceed your cost investment, they are not taxable as income until after they equal your cost investment.

EXAMPLES—

1. Starting July 1, 1982, you receive a pension annuity of $300 a month for the rest of your life. You contributed $9000 to the policy; your company paid the balance. Because payments will equal or exceed your cost within three years, payments received before January 1, 1985, are not taxable income.

Payments in	Total
1982 (six months)	$1800
1983	3600
1984	3600
	$9000

2. Same facts as above except you contributed only $6000 to the policy.

Payments in	Total
1982 (six months)	$1800
1983	3600
1984 (two months)	600
	$6000

Taxable payments (ten months) reported in 1984 total $3000.

After you have received payments equaling your investment, all future payments are ordinary income.

If you will not recover your cost within three years after your pension starts, follow the rules discussed below.

An increase in the amount of payments during the three-year period does not permit use of the three-year rule if you could not have used it initially.

An employee is taxed on the full value of a nonforfeitable annuity contract which his or her employer buys if the employer does not have a qualified pension plan. Tax is imposed in the year the policy is purchased.

You may receive benefits from more than one program under a single trust or plan of an employer or from several trusts or plans. Check with your former employer if you are covered by more than one pension or annuity contract. If so, you have to account for each contract separately even though benefits are included in one check.

Variable annuity. The three-year cost rules apply to periodic payments under a variable annuity contract financed by you and your employer. To determine whether you will recover your cost within three years, multiply the amount of the first periodic payment by the number of periodic payments to be made within the three years beginning on the date of its receipt.

How annuities are taxed if you cannot use the three-year rule

If you cannot use the three-year rule to report your annuity, you must follow six steps to determine which part of each payment is taxable and which part is tax free.

1. Figure your investment in the annuity, as discussed above.

2. Find your expected return. This is the total of all the payments you are to receive. If the payments are to be made to you for life, your expected return is figured by multiplying the amount of the annual payment by a multiple based on your life expectancy as of the annuity starting date. These multiples are listed in tables published by the Treasury. The tables are available from your local district director, or you can write to your insurance company, requesting the amount of your expected return. Below is the table to use when payments are made to one person for life and cease on that person's death.

Find your age at the birthday nearest your annuity starting date in the proper column—"Male" or "Female." Then look opposite your age to find the proper multiple. You then multiply this figure by the total annuity payments you are to receive in one full year. If you have a monthly annuity, you multiply the figure by 12 times the monthly payments. The product is your expected return.

If the payments are for a fixed number of years (as in an endowment contract), find your expected return by multiplying your annual payments by the number of years you are to receive them.

Ages		Multi-	Ages		Multi-	Ages		Multi-
Male	Female	ples	Male	Female	ples	Male	Female	ples
6	11	65.0	41	46	33.0	76	81	9.1
7	12	64.1	42	47	32.1	77	82	8.7
8	13	63.2	43	48	31.2	78	83	8.3
9	14	62.3	44	49	30.4	79	84	7.8
10	15	61.4	45	50	29.6	80	85	7.5
11	16	60.4	46	51	28.7	81	86	7.1
12	17	59.5	47	52	27.9	82	87	6.7
13	18	58.6	48	53	27.1	83	88	6.3
14	19	57.7	49	54	26.3	84	89	6.0
15	20	56.7	50	55	25.5	85	90	5.7
16	21	55.8	51	56	24.7	86	91	5.4
17	22	54.9	52	57	24.0	87	92	5.1
18	23	53.9	53	58	23.2	88	93	4.8
19	24	53.0	54	59	22.4	89	94	4.5
20	25	52.1	55	60	21.7	90	95	4.2
21	26	51.1	56	61	21.0	91	96	4.0
22	27	50.2	57	62	20.3	92	97	3.7
23	28	49.3	58	63	19.6	93	98	3.5
24	29	48.3	59	64	18.9	94	99	3.3
25	30	47.4	60	65	18.2	95	100	3.1
26	31	46.5	61	66	17.5	96	101	2.9
27	32	45.6	62	67	16.9	97	102	2.7
28	33	44.6	63	68	16.2	98	103	2.5
29	34	43.7	64	69	15.6	99	104	2.3
30	35	42.8	65	70	15.0	100	105	2.1
31	36	41.9	66	71	14.4	101	106	1.9
32	37	41.0	67	72	13.8	102	107	1.7
33	38	40.0	68	73	13.2	103	108	1.5
34	39	39.1	69	74	12.6	104	109	1.3
35	40	38.2	70	75	12.1	105	110	1.2
36	41	37.3	71	76	11.6	106	111	1.0
37	42	36.5	72	77	11.0	107	112	.8
38	43	35.6	73	78	10.5	108	113	.7
39	44	34.7	74	79	10.1	109	114	.6
40	45	33.8	75	80	9.6	110	115	.5
						111	116	0

3. Divide the investment in contract (step 1) by the expected return (step 2). This will give you the percentage of your yearly annuity payments which is tax free. The percentage remains the same for the remaining years of the annuity.

4. Find your total annuity receipts for the year. For example, you received ten monthly payments, as your annuity began in March. Your total is the monthly payment multiplied by ten.

5. Multiply the percentage in step 3 by the total in step 4. The resulting amount is the nontaxable portion (or excludable amount) of your annuity payments.

6. Subtract the amounts in step 5 from the amount figured in step 4. This is the part of your annuity subject to tax for the year. Here is an example of how an employee who would not recover his or her cost within three years must report retirement pay:

EXAMPLE—

Jones was 66 years old on March 14, 1982. On April 1 he received his first monthly annuity check of $100 covering his payment for March. His annuity starting date is March 1, 1982. Looking at the table for a male at age 66, Jones finds the multiple 14.4. Jones multiplies 14.4 by $1200 ($100 a month for a year) to find his expected return of $17,280. Assume the annuity cost Jones $12,960. He divides his expected return into the investment in the contract (the cost) and determines his exclusion percentage, 75%. Thereafter, in every year for the rest of his life, Jones receives 75% of his annuity payments tax free and is taxed on 25%. For 1982 Jones reports his annuity income as follows:

Amount received	$900
Amount excludable	675
Taxable portion	$225

For 1983 and later years Jones will receive annuity payments for the full year. The amount received will be $1200; the amount excludable is $900; the taxable portion is $300.

How Civil Service retirement pay is taxed

Almost all U.S. Civil Service retirees use the three-year rule since they usually receive annuity benefits sufficient to recover their cost within three years after they retire.

While you worked for the federal government, contributions to the Civil Service retirement fund were withheld from your pay. These contributions represent your cost. Also, if you repaid to the retirement fund amounts that you previously had withdrawn, or paid into the fund to receive full credit for certain uncovered service, the entire amount you paid, including that designated as interest, is part of your cost. You may not claim an interest deduction for any amount designated as interest.

The Civil Service annuity statement you received when your annuity was approved shows your "total contributions" to the retirement fund (your cost) and the "monthly rate" of your annuity benefit. The monthly rate is the rate before adjustment for health benefits coverage and life insurance, if any. To determine whether you will recover your cost within three years, multiply your initial monthly rate by 36. If the result equals or exceeds your cost, you must use the three-year rule. If you will not recover your cost within the three-year period, follow the six-step approach outlined above.

An increase in the monthly rate of your annuity resulting from a cost-of-living increase does not affect the method of reporting your annuity on your tax return. If you determine that you must use the three-year rule, your entire annuity, including the increase, is fully taxable after you have received payments equaling your cost. If when you received your first annuity payment you determined that you may not use the three-year rule, a later increase in your monthly rate will not enable you to use it. A future increase in a Civil Service pension to the retiree or his survivor is not treated as annuity income but is reported in full as miscellaneous income and is not reduced by the exclusion ratio. However, an increase effective on or before a survivor's Civil Service annuity commences must be taken into account in computing the expected return or in determining the aggregate amount receivable under the annuity.

If you retired during the past year and filed your application for retirement late or are entitled to accrued payments because your application was processed late, you may receive a lump-sum payment representing the unpaid accrued monthly installments for the period before your regular monthly payments begin. If the lump sum is less than your cost of the annuity, you determine whether the three-year rule applies as explained above. Disregarding the lump sum, multiply the monthly rate of your annuity by 36; if that amount plus the lump sum equals or exceeds your cost, you must use the three-year rule. In determining your tax for the year under the three-year rule, the lump sum is treated as a tax-free recovery of part of your cost. If the lump sum exceeds your cost of the annuity, the excess is fully taxable. Also, all the regular monthly annuity payments you receive thereafter are fully taxable.

A lump-sum payment for accrued annual leave received upon retirement is not part of your annuity. It is treated as a salary payment and is taxable as ordinary income.

If you made voluntary contributions to the retirement fund, you report the portion of your annuity attributable to the voluntary contributions as a separate annuity taxable under the six-step method.

If you made voluntary contributions, an information return which you receive each year will state the portion of your monthly payments attributable to your voluntary contributions.

How beneficiaries of deceased employees report annuity payments

A pension annuity paid to you as the beneficiary of a deceased employee (or an owner who dies after 1983) may qualify for a death benefit exclusion, up to $5000. The amount of the exclusion is added to the cost of the annuity in calculating the investment in the contract as of the annuity starting date. Thus if the employee's contribution plus the death benefit exclusion will be recovered within three years of the annuity starting date, you report the annuity payments under the three-year rule.

EXAMPLE—

An employee contributed $9000 to his annuity. When he died, his widow was entitled to $3000 a year and his two children to $1000 a year each. In the first three years they will receive a total of $15,000. Of this amount, $14,000 is considered a tax-free recovery of the employee's cost (cost of $9000 plus $5000 death benefit). In the first two years the widow and the children exclude the full amount of their pension benefits ($10,000). In the third year the remaining $4000 to be received tax free is allocated according to the ratio of benefits received by each person; the widow receives $2400 tax free (60% of the remaining $4000) and each child receives $800 tax free (20% of $4000).

The $5000 exclusion may not be added to the investment if the deceased had received any payment under a joint and survivor contract after reaching retirement age.

If after taking the $5000 exclusion into account in computing the investment in the contract the three-year rule is not applicable (because the contract investment exceeds the return of the first three years), the beneficiary follows the six-step method to compute taxable income. If the annuity is payable over the lifetime of the beneficiary, actuarial tables are used to determine the expected return on the contract. Ask the company paying the annuity to give you these amounts. The maximum amount of the death benefit exclusion is fixed at $5000, without regard to the number of beneficiaries or the number of employers funding pension payments.

Military personnel allowed tax exclusion on annuity election

If, when you retire from the military, you elect to receive reduced retirement pay to provide an annuity for your spouse or certain child beneficiaries, you do not report that part of your retirement pay used to fund the annuity.

EXAMPLE—

You are eligible to receive retirement pay of $500 a month. You elect a joint and survivor annuity paying you $400 a month and $200 to your spouse on your death. You report $400 a month for tax purposes during your lifetime, rather than the $500. On your death, your spouse generally will report the full $200 a month received as income.

If you received retirement pay before 1966 and elected reduced benefits, you reported more retirement pay than you actually received. In this case, amounts attributed to the reduction in retirement pay reported in prior years offset retirement pay received in 1966 and later years.

If you elected to receive veteran's benefits instead of some or all of your retirement pay, you may have been required to deposit with the U.S. Treasury an amount equal to the reduction for the annuity. If so, you do not report retirement pay until it equals the amount deposited.

If all the retired person's consideration for the contract (previously taxed reductions) has not been offset against retirement income at the time of death, the beneficiary is entitled to a tax break. The beneficiary excludes all payments under the contract until the exclusions equal the remaining consideration for the contract not previously excluded by the deceased. As soon as this amount is excluded, the beneficiary reports all later payments as income.

The $5000 death benefit exclusion is treated as a cost investment to be added to the spouse's annuity contract if the serviceman retired because of disability and died before reaching retirement age.

Are your retirement benefits protected from the claims of creditors and ex-spouses?

Retirement benefits, whether accrued in a company plan or saved through your IRA, make up a significant source of funds. If you are experiencing financial difficulty or if you are in the process of negotiating a divorce settlement, you may face the question of whether this source can be tapped. The answer is not clear-cut.

All qualified plans are required to contain an "anti-alienation provision" which prohibits a participant from assigning or alienating plan benefits. The reason for such a provision is to ensure that the benefits are generally not subject to attachment, garnishment, levy, execution, or other legal or equitable process. There are some exceptions.

Benefits are not shielded from enforcement of a federal tax levy or collection by the federal government on a judgment for an unpaid tax assessment.

Federal law does not prevent a creditor from attaching a regular IRA account. Recently, a New York court held that a judgment creditor can attach an IRA account held by a bank-trustee. Although the IRA cannot be assigned by the owner, it can be attached by the creditor. While New York law exempts from satisfaction-of-judgment procedures the assets of a trust set up by one person for the benefit of another, the exemption does not apply to an IRA since the trust grantor and beneficiary are the same person. When an IRA account is taken by a creditor, the IRA owner must report the distribution as income. Further, if the owner is not age 59½ or over or disabled, he or she is subject to a 10% penalty for a premature withdrawal.

An IRA bond by its terms may be exempt from attachment, at least until the owner is age 59½. Similarly, an IRA annuity may be exempt since the policy, by its terms, is nontransferable.

The Bankruptcy Act of 1978 provides that, under federal law, an employee's rights under a qualified pension or profit-sharing plan are exempt from the bankruptcy estate to the extent reasonably necessary to provide for the support of the bankrupt or his dependents. Thus there is no absolute exemption under federal law. Moreover, states have their own bankruptcy rules which may apply. A bankruptcy court in Wisconsin has held that Keogh plan contributions were not exempt from the bankrupt's estate under federal law. Similarly, a bankruptcy court in Tennessee held that contributions to a defined-contribution Keogh plan were not exempt under either Tennessee or federal law.

Marital actions. Whether ex-spouses have rights to their former spouse's pension benefits is a troublesome area. The issue may become critical when support or alimony obligations are in arrears. Courts have almost unanimously upheld a spouse's right to share in the employee-spouse's benefits. Such a holding is based on the belief that the antialienation provision was designed to protect spouses and other dependents. For example, one appeals court has upheld a garnishment order that required distribution of a former husband's accrued pension benefits to satisfy alimony and child support obligations. In marital settlements, a vested interest in a pension plan has been viewed by some courts as a marital asset. For example, a Michigan court held that a husband's 70% vested pension was a marital asset capable of being valued and included in the settlement.

Withholding tax on pension benefits

Beginning in 1983 pension benefits and IRA distributions are automatically subject to withholding. For many recipients this will avoid the need to pay estimated tax. However, if you choose, you may elect to avoid withholding.

Withholding on annuities and other periodic payments exceeding $5400 annually will be based on the wage withholding tables. For lump-sum payments, a special withholding table will be used to take into account the ten-year averaging method.

Payors unable to comply with the withholding requirements may be granted an exemption by the IRS until July 1, 1983 if there is a plan to comply by that date. No civil or criminal penalties for failure to withhold will be imposed before July 1, 1983 if withholdings from later 1983 payments compensate for pre-July underwithholdings.

Chapter 9
TAX-FREE ROLLOVERS

THE transfer of a lump-sum distribution to a qualified pension plan or IRA is called a rollover. A rollover allows you to defer tax on lump-sum distributions.

Is a rollover advisable when you retire?

A rollover does not allow you to avoid payment of tax. It merely postpones payment to some future date. The decision to make a rollover involves an evaluation of present and future needs as well as the tax consequences of the rollover. If you need the funds immediately, perhaps to buy a retirement home or start a business for your retirement years, you will not roll over the distribution. If you receive a lump-sum distribution because your plan terminates but you were not a plan participant for at least five years, you may not use ten-year averaging and should make a rollover to avoid immediate tax. Even if you do qualify for ten-year averaging but do not have a pressing need for the funds, you may consider a rollover, weighing the tax consequences of postponing tax through rollovers with the payment of immediate tax using ten-year averaging. This comparison is examined further in Chapter 8.

EXAMPLES—

1. In 1982 you receive a lump-sum distribution of $100,000. You made no contribution to the sum. If you decide not to roll the amount over to an IRA, the tax under ten-year averaging is $17,200, leaving you $82,800. If you rolled over the amount to an IRA, you would defer tax but lose the right to use ten-year averaging. This might prove costly if an emergency required you to withdraw the entire amount from the IRA. For exam-

ple, two years after you roll over you need the funds from the IRA account, which has grown to $125,000. If the amount was subject to the following tax rates, you would net as follows:

Tax rate	Net
25%	$93,750
30%	$87,500
40%	$76,000
50%	$62,500

If you had not made the rollover and had invested the $82,800 in tax exempts paying around 12%, your fund would have been about $102,600 in two years. Here, the better choice would have been not to roll over.

Assume you retire at 65 and do not currently need the $100,000. You roll it over. When you reach age 70 the value of the fund is $176,000. If you withdraw the amount as a lump sum, you net as follows:

Tax rate	Net
25%	$132,000
30%	$123,200
40%	$105,600
50%	$ 88,000

If you had not rolled over the $100,000, you would have netted $82,800 which, if invested in tax exempts returning 12%, would provide $145,920 at age 70.

2. Assume you retire at age 60 and receive $100,000. If you decide not to roll over, the net amount of $82,800 invested at 12% tax exempt will grow in ten years to $257,000. If you roll over $100,000 at 12%, it will grow to $310,000 at age 70. If at that time you withdraw the amount as a lump sum, you would net the following:

Tax rate	Net
25%	$232,500
30%	$217,000
40%	$186,000
50%	$155,000

Based on the above projections, it is generally unwise to roll over if you are planning to take your account in a lump sum. On the other hand, a rollover may prove more advantageous if you allow the fund to accumulate tax free and then withdraw the fund over your life expectancy. However, even here, paying the tax immediately may return more if you invest in instruments yielding a substantial tax-free return.

You do not have to make a rollover of your entire account; you may roll over part of the distribution and keep part of it. The rolled-over portion is tax free. The amount not rolled over is currently taxable. However, because you have rolled over a portion of the total funds, you may not use special ten-year averaging or capital gain treatment for the taxable amount even though you could have used these methods if you had not made a rollover.

Rules for making a tax-free rollover into an IRA or a qualified plan

A lump-sum distribution from a qualified plan is not taxable if within 60 days it is transferred in whole or in part to a qualified plan of your new employer or to an IRA which you set up on your own behalf.

To make a tax-free rollover from a qualified plan to an IRA or another qualified plan, your lump-sum distribution must meet these tests:

1. The distribution must be all that is due you under the plan. That is, if your employer's plan uses more than one trust, you must receive a distribution of all that is due you from each trust.

2. The payment or payments must be made within one of your taxable years.

3. The distribution must be made because you are separated from service, reach age 59½, or the plan has been terminated, or in the case of a profit-sharing plan, there has been a complete discontinuance of contributions.

You may make a rollover even though you do not qualify for ten-year averaging because you were not a plan participant for five years before retirement.

You may make a rollover to an IRA even though you are age 70½ provided you begin to take minimum distributions as discussed in Chapter 3.

A surviving spouse may roll over to an IRA a lump-sum distribution paid on the death of a spouse or upon termination of a qualified retirement plan. Such a rollover may not include benefits attributable to the deceased's nondeductible contributions to the plan. The distribution may not be rolled over to a qualified plan of the surviving spouse's current employer.

If you receive property, such as your employer's stock, as part of your distribution, you must roll over the same property or sell it and roll over the sales proceeds as discussed later in this chapter.

The amount you roll over may not include your nondeductible contributions to the qualified plan. However, if beginning in 1982 you make deductible voluntary contributions to your employer's plan, you must include your contributions in a tax-free rollover.

You may not claim a deduction for your rollover contribution to an IRA even if you did not use up your IRA contribution limit for the year.

An IRA account may be used as a conduit between two company plans. The funds in the IRA account may be transferred to another qualified plan of a company for which you work, provided the plan of your new employer accepts rollovers. The IRA account must consist of only the assets (or proceeds from the sale of such assets) previously distributed from the first qualified plan and income earned on the account. You may not contribute to the account set up as a conduit. If you are not immediately employed or are employed by a company not having a qualified plan, you may set up another IRA account to which you may make annual contributions. In such a case you will have two accounts: one consisting of the assets (or proceeds from the sale of such assets) of the plan of your prior employer and the other of your own contributions.

EXAMPLE—

You leave your employer and receive a lump-sum distribution of $5000 from his qualified plan to which you did not contribute. You place the amount in an IRA account. Four years later you start work for another company that has a qualified plan. The new plan permits you to transfer the assets of the IRA to the plan. You must make the transfer within 60 days after closing the IRA account.

When the distribution is substantial, you may wish to divide it and put portions into different investments. Diversification is permissible. There is no limit on the number of rollover accounts you may have. A lump-sum distribution may be rolled over to several IRAs or retirement annuities.

Rollover of annuities for employees of tax-exempt groups and schools. If you participate in a tax-sheltered annuity program, you may roll over a lump-sum distribution to an IRA.

Changing a rollover election

Suppose you make a rollover but later decide that you would have been better off paying tax currently using ten-year averaging. Can you undo your rollover election? If you act quickly, you may reverse your move without penalty. In a private letter ruling, the IRS allowed a retired person to change to ten-year averaging after making a rollover.

EXAMPLE—

Smith received a lump-sum distribution from his company plan which he rolled over to an IRA account. He was over 59½ and started to make small withdrawals from the IRA when he realized that he had made the wrong tax election. Withdrawals from the IRA incurred a higher tax cost than the tax he would have incurred if he had not made the rollover and applied the ten-year averaging method to the distribution. The IRS ruled that he may file an amended return for the year of the distribution and elect to compute his tax under the ten-year averaging method as long as the time for filing an amended return had not expired for that year.

To avoid tax penalties on undoing a rollover, you must close out your account before the due date of the return for the year in which you received the distribution. Income earned on the rollover account must be reported as ordinary income. A change may be made within three years from the due date (plus extensions) of the return for the year of distribution, but tax penalties on the withdrawal may not be avoided unless the account is closed before due date of the return for the year of distribution. Closing out the IRA account may also result in a bank interest penalty for premature withdrawals.

Rollover of proceeds from sale of property received in lump-sum distribution

A lump-sum distribution from a qualified plan may include property, such as stock. If you plan to roll over the distribution, you may find that a bank may not want to take the property. If you sell the property for this or another reason, you may roll over the sale proceeds to an IRA as long as the sale and rollover take place within 60 days of the receipt of the distribution. If you roll over all the proceeds, no tax is incurred on any gain realized on the sale. Similarly, if you realize a loss it is not deductible. The proceeds are treated as part of the distribution. If you make a partial rollover, you incur tax on the retained proceeds, and in reporting the taxable amount you allocate between ordinary income and capital gain elements according to the following special formulas.

If you receive cash and property in your distribution and you sell the property but make a partial rollover, you must designate the amount of cash to be treated as part of the rollover. The designation must be made by the time for filing your return (plus any extensions) and is irrevocable. If you do not make a timely designation, the allocation between cash and proceeds is made on a ratable basis.

The distribution to the extent of your contributions to the plan may not be rolled over to an IRA. See Treasury regulations for the effect of employee contributions on an allocation.

Rollovers of IRAs

You may transfer assets tax free from one IRA to another. Such transfers are treated as a distribution of the assets from your old plan to you. To avoid tax on the transfer, these tests must be met: (1) You must transfer the amount you receive from your old plan to the new plan within 60 days. (2) A tax-free rollover may occur only once within a one-year period.

If you make another rollover within the same one-year period, you are taxed on the plan assets as they are distributed to you.

As long as funds are not distributed to you, a transfer or reinvestment is not considered a rollover. Thus if your CD matures and you direct the bank to renew the CD for another term, you have not made a rollover. Similarly, a transfer of funds from one bank to another may not constitute a rollover subject to the one-year restriction.

EXAMPLE—

Smith sets up an IRA at Bank A. He later instructs Bank A to transfer the funds to Bank B. The transfer from Bank A to Bank B is not subject to the one-year restriction on rollovers because there was no payment or distribution of the funds to Smith.

According to proposed Treasury regulations, the one-year rule applies to each IRA you have. For example, you have an IRA at your local bank as well as an IRA annuity with your insurance company. In 1982 you make a tax-free rollover of your annuity to a mutual fund IRA. You may also roll over your bank IRA in 1982.

You have not made a tax-free rollover if you take a distribution from your IRA and use it to buy an endowment policy. The distribution is included in your gross income and is subject to tax.

Partial rollover. You need not make a complete rollover of the distribution to ensure tax-free treatment. For distributions after 1982 you may make a partial rollover. The part rolled over is not taxed; the part of the distribution you retain is taxable.

Tax-free transfer of an IRA because of divorce

A spouse may transfer his IRA account tax free to an IRA account of his former spouse. As long as the transfer is made under a valid divorce decree or written agreement incident to the divorce, there are no tax consequences to either party, provided the transferred account, policy, or bond is maintained in the name of the spouse who receives it.

Chapter 10
SOCIAL SECURITY

SOCIAL Security is a government program designed to provide workers and their dependents with tax-free retirement funds and other benefits. Recently, there has been much publicity on the fiscal stability and future of Social Security. The underlying problem is that in the coming years there will be fewer workers to support an ever-growing number of retirees. Nevertheless, Social Security is likely to continue with some changes by Congress.

The Social Security program provides four types of benefits:

1. Retirement benefits for workers and for spouses and dependent children of retirees. These benefits begin at age 65, or at a reduced level at age 62.

2. Survivor's benefits for the spouse, minor children, and dependent elderly parents of a worker who dies.

3. Disability benefits for a worker who is unable to work for an extended period. Benefits are also paid to the spouse and children of a disabled worker.

4. Medical insurance (Medicare) beginning at age 65 and for disabled workers who have been receiving disability payments for at least 24 months.

Qualifying for benefits

You must work for a required period of time in covered employment to obtain insured status. The required time depends on your age or the date of your retirement, death, or disability. There are two types of coverage, currently insured status and fully insured status. If you have worked for at least ten years in covered employment, you are fully insured, regardless of your age. If you have not, you may still qualify under one of several tests which give insured status even if you have less than ten years in covered employment.

Currently insured status. This protection is designed to help families of those who die without having enough coverage to qualify for retirement benefits.

If you are currently insured at the time you die, survivor benefits are payable to:

Your unmarried children (or dependent grandchildren whose parents are dead or disabled) if under 18 or disabled, regardless of their ages.

Your spouse (or divorced spouse), if caring for your child under 18.

Also payable under the currently insured status are lump-sum death benefits to a spouse or eligible child.

Fully insured status. If you have fully insured status, you and your family may receive retirement and disability benefits, and your family also receives protection in case of your death. Retirement benefits are payable to the following:

The insured worker, age 62 or over.
Spouse or divorced spouse, age 62 or over.
Spouse, any age, if caring for child under age 18.
Children or grandchildren (if qualified as above).

In addition, survivor's benefits are paid as under the *currently insured* section, and *fully insured status* may also provide survivor benefits to:

Widow, widower, or divorced spouse, age 60 or over; earlier if disabled.
Dependent parent, age 62 or over.

Working wives should note that they have their own earnings record and can collect benefits on their own. They need not wait until their husbands retire to collect benefits. Working spouses receive the higher of the worker's benefit or the spousal benefit, but not both.

A divorced spouse may collect on the account of his or her former retired spouse (the insured worker) if the marriage lasted ten years or longer before ending in divorce. If the insured worker remarries, the divorced spouse may still collect on his or her account, even if the insured's new spouse is also collecting. But if the nonworking divorced spouse remarries, he or she may not collect on the former spouse's account. The remarried spouse can collect only on the account of the new spouse. However, if the second marriage ends in divorce after ten years, he or she may collect on the account of either former spouse if both former spouses were insured. If the second marriage ends in divorce in less than ten years, he or she may collect only on the account of the first spouse. But if the insured spouse of the second marriage dies after one year, the uninsured spouse may collect on the account of the deceased.

EXAMPLES—

1. Paul and Joan Brown divorce after 12 years of marriage. Joan does not work. Paul remarries but Joan does not. When Paul retires, both Joan and Paul's second wife may collect on his account.

2. Same as above but following the divorce from Paul, Joan marries Sam. She may collect only on Sam's account. If the second marriage ends in divorce after ten years, she may collect on either Paul's or Sam's account. If the second marriage had not lasted ten years, Joan would have been able to collect only on Paul's account.

A divorced person who takes care of a former spouse's children is eligible for benefits when the former spouse dies or retires, even if the marriage did not last ten years. Children of a divorced couple are eligible for dependents' or survivors' benefits on the record of either parent. Their benefits are not affected by the custody or support arrangements of their divorced parents.

Benefits to a widow or widower usually end if he or she remarries. However, this rule does not apply if the widow or widower is age 60 or older when the second marriage takes place. An individual may receive a benefit on the account of the new spouse if it would be larger than the widow's or widower's benefit.

Students age 18 to 22 who receive Social Security benefits

because a parent is disabled, retired, or deceased may receive benefits through their college years if they had been receiving benefits and began college by May 1982. However, students' benefits have been reduced and are being phased out; they will end after April 1985.

There is a ceiling on the amount of benefits that may be paid on one worker's account. This limit is calculated using a formula based on the worker's earnings.

Keep a record of credits. You should keep a record of your earnings and payments of Social Security taxes (FICA). The Social Security Administration has been criticized for not keeping up with workers' earnings records. Do not risk a problem by ignoring your record. At least once every three years, you should mail Form SSA–7004, Request for Statement of Earnings, to the Social Security Administration, P.O. Box 56, Baltimore, MD 21203. This form is available at your local Social Security office and at the headquarters in Baltimore. You will receive a response in about six weeks. Compare it with your records.

Social Security forms state that if you wait more than three years, three months, and 15 days after an error is discovered to request a correction, a change may not be possible. The agency waived the deadline in 1981 since it had fallen behind in its recordkeeping, but you should still try to correct any errors immediately.

Applying for Social Security retirement benefits

You should make your application to collect benefits at the local Social Security office three months before your 62nd or 65th birthday, depending on the year you plan to retire. This allows enough time for your claim to be processed and to locate all necessary information.

You cannot collect Social Security benefits without applying for them. The government is not obligated to remind you of your rights or benefits. You must contact your local Social Security office for information and to begin the collection process. It is advisable to call before going to the office so you will know which personal papers, such as proof of your age, you must bring with you.

Payment of benefits

Social Security checks are mailed to reach a beneficiary on the third of the month following the benefit month. That is, you receive your January check on February 3. When a husband and wife are both receiving benefits, they usually receive one check for the total amount. If you prefer, you may request separate checks. For your convenience and safety, you may have your check deposited directly in your account at a bank or thrift by filling out Standard Form 1199, Authorization for Deposit of Social Security Payments, available at your financial institution.

Estimating retirement benefits

How much you receive from Social Security at retirement depends on your earnings history. For years there was a guaranteed minimum benefit, but legislation in 1981 ended this minimum for persons retiring in 1982 and later years.

The amount of your benefit may be adjusted each year to account for increases in the cost of living. If the Consumer Price Index rises 3% or more, benefits will be increased. The adjustment currently begins with the July check. There have been increases every year since 1976 when this provision went into effect, as seen in the following chart:

AVERAGE MONTHLY BENEFITS

Year	Retired worker[b]	Spouse	Children
1977	$242.98	$123.07	$94.85
1978	263.19	132.77	105.69
1979	294.27	148.36	119.80
1980	341.41	171.95	140.49
1981	385.97	194.75	161.39
1982[a]	387.08	195.41	163.19

[a] As of March 1982.
[b] Average includes retirees age 62 and older.

If you are age 55 or older, your local Social Security office can provide an estimate of your retirement benefits. You may request a pamphlet entitled "Estimating Your Social Security Retirement Check" at a local office. However, determining your own monthly benefit is difficult because the formula provided is very complicated.

Below is a projection of benefits for individuals retiring at ages 62 and 65 in upcoming years.

AVERAGE MONTHLY BENEFITS

Year	Retired worker age 62	Retired worker age 65
1983	$424.08	$575.92
1984	452.67	589.08
1985	486.67	616.92
1986	524.08	663.75
1987	558.50	696.17
1988	595.75	735.75
1989	634.17	781.75
1990	674.50	824.17

Social Security and retirement planning

For many, Social Security is a necessary mainstay of their retirement income. However, Social Security benefits can only cover some basic needs, and thus should not be the only source of funds in your retirement plans. A substantial savings account, a retirement account, income from investments, and in some cases, work after retirement should supplement Social Security benefits.

Should you retire early? Your decision must take into account your overall financial picture, as well as your personal goals and work opportunities. We consider here only the effect of your decision on Social Security benefits. If you choose to retire early, you may do so and begin to receive benefits at age 62 (generally in the month following your birthday). However, the amount of your monthly benefits is permanently reduced.

The reduction is figured by a formula based on the number of months before age 65 that you retire. If you retire at the earliest age, 62, your monthly benefit is reduced by about 20%. If you live until age 77, retiring at age 62 means that you will receive more total benefits from the system than if you delay retirement until 65. Age 77 is the break-even point at which it makes no overall difference whether you opted for early retirement. Beyond age 77, you receive more benefits if you wait until age 65 to retire.

Should you delay retirement? If you do not retire at age 65, you increase the retirement benefit you will receive when you retire. For those born in 1916 or earlier, the increase is 1% per year for each year of delayed retirement; for those born in 1917 or later, the increase is 3% a year. No additional credit accrues in the month you reach 72 and thereafter.

What is the effect of working after you begin to receive retirement benefits? If you are 65 or older but under 72, you can earn $6000 in 1982 without losing benefits. If you are under 65 for the entire year, you can earn $4440 in 1982 without losing benefits. Once you earn more than these amounts, benefits are reduced. For every $2 you earn, you lose $1 in benefits. A special month rule applies in the year you reach retirement age so your earnings will be limited only in the months after you reach 65. Earnings include self-employment income.

For those age 72 or over (age 70 beginning in 1983), benefits are not affected by earnings. Thus you can work, earn any amount, and receive full Social Security benefits.

As long as you continue to work, you pay Social Security taxes on your earnings, regardless of your age.

What is the effect of income from other sources? You may receive any amount of income from sources other than work, for example, from private pensions or investments, without affecting your Social Security retirement benefits.

You may be affected if your Social Security benefit is through your spouse or parent and you did not work and if you are receiving a benefit from a federal or state pension plan. Your Social Security benefit may be reduced by the amount of the pension. However, this rule does not apply to most people who were eligible to receive a government pension before December 1982.

Medicare and additional health insurance

Retirees spend substantially more on health care than younger workers. When planning for your future expenses, health insurance is a necessity for which you must provide. While Medicare covers some charges, as explained in the following pages, rising costs in the Medicare program which must be borne by the patient weigh heavily on the retiree with diminished income. If your company has no retiree health insurance coverage to supplement Medicare, you must buy individual policies to help cover the gaps in both Parts A and B. As of July 1, 1982, the federal government will certify those so-called medigap policies that meet federal standards. Be sure to obtain approved coverage; many retirees have been victimized in the past by inadequate, unnecessary, and high-priced policies. You can obtain a free booklet, "Guide to Health Insurance for People With Medicare," by writing to the Office of Beneficiary Services, Health Care Financing Administration, 648 East Highrise, 6325 Security Blvd., Baltimore, MD 21207.

When you shop for a policy, find out first whether your employer provides a health insurance plan to retired workers or whether the policy you had through your job may be converted to an individual policy upon retirement. Blue Cross/Blue Shield policies are often convertible. Continuing the same policy has advantages: there is no lapse in coverage and you do not have to worry about "preexisting" conditions.

Many medigap policies are designed to coordinate benefits with your Medicare coverage. However, read such policies carefully; some costs will still not be covered. For example, most supplementary policies, like Medicare, do not pay for regular checkups. Other policies pay you cash but do not pay particular bills. While the cash payment sounds appealing in advertisements, these policies are not usually the best value for your money. Also, avoid "dread disease" policies which insure only against a particular illness, such as cancer. A regular policy offering broad coverage provides better protection.

Your state may offer additional health care assistance through a medicaid program, but you may be required to meet income qualifications to participate.

Medicare coverage

When you apply for Social Security benefits at age 65, your enrollment in Part A Medicare, covering hospitalization, is automatic. At the same time you may enroll in Part B, covering medical-surgical expenses, for which there is a monthly premium, currently $12.20, that is usually deducted from your monthly Social Security payments. Even if you are not yet retired, you become eligible for Medicare at age 65 and should take advantage of it. A worker's spouse is eligible for Medicare when he or she reaches age 65.

If you do not choose to enroll in Part B in the initial enrollment period (three months before to three months after the month in which you turn 65) you may enroll later, but your premium would be higher than if you had enrolled initially. Also, if you enroll in Medicare Part B and then drop out, you are subject to a higher premium if you choose to enroll again later. You pay this higher premium the rest of your life.

There is no premium for Part A, Hospital Insurance, if you meet Social Security work requirements. (If you are not eligible for benefits, you may still obtain Part A coverage by paying a monthly premium, now $113.) In 1982, there is a deductible of $260 ($304 in 1983) for the first 60 days of hospitalization. From the 61st to the 90th day you pay co-insurance of $65 ($76 in 1983) a day. You also have a lifetime reserve of 60 days for which there is a daily charge of $130 ($152 in 1983).

Part A also pays for nursing services (except private-duty nursing), usual drugs and supplies for hospital patients, and other services and treatments furnished by the hospital. Most hospital expenses are covered, but Part A does not pay for the first three pints of whole blood. However, if friends and relatives donate an equivalent amount of blood, you will not be charged. Nonmedical hospital costs, such as a private room or a telephone, are not covered.

A patient transferred to a qualified nursing home after three days of hospitalization pays $32.50 ($38 in 1983) a day after

20 days in the home. Note that the only kind of nursing home covered by Medicare is a skilled nursing facility. Residential nursing homes are not covered. Home health services for patients confined to their homes are covered by Part A. These include the part-time services of a home health aide, intermittent nursing care, and physical, occupational, or speech therapy.

Part B, Supplementary Medical Insurance, partially covers the services of physicians and surgeons and certain medical and health services. It pays 80% of "reasonable charges." The patient is liable for an annual deductible of $75, the remaining 20% of costs, and any amounts considered above "reasonable charges." For Part B, a doctor can choose whether to accept the assignment, that is, if he or she will accept Medicare's reasonable charges as his or her fee. If the doctor agrees, Medicare pays 80%, you pay 20%, and the bill is considered paid in full. If your doctor does not accept the assignment, Medicare still pays 80% according to its schedule of reasonable fees, but you must pay the difference between Medicare's payment and your doctor's actual charge.

Part B also pays for durable medical equipment, such as crutches or a hospital bed. It does not pay for equipment inappropriate to the home and items that are considered personal conveniences. Check with your local Medicare office about whether specific items would be covered. Also, find out whether it would be more practical to rent rather than buy such equipment.

Benefit period

When you review your Medicare benefits, you will see the term "benefit period." For example, Part A covers the cost of 90 days in the hospital during a single benefit period. Generally, a benefit period means the length of your illness. It applies only to Part A coverage, not to Part B. As defined by Medicare, it begins on the day you enter the hospital and continues until you have been out of the hospital or skilled nursing facility for 60 consecutive days. There is no limit to the number of benefit periods you may have, and you pay a deductible once for each period. The problem with the benefit period concept is that an individual may run out of coverage if a long illness strikes. If you are hospitalized for more than 90 days, you must begin to use up your lifetime reserve of 60 days or lose coverage. If you use all your reserve days in one illness, your Part A Medicare coverage ends for that period. When you leave a hospital or skilled nursing facility after an illness, you must wait 60 days before beginning a new benefit period. Most hospital stays do not extend more than 90 days, but long-term illness is one area where Medicare coverage falls short.

Filing claims

For Part A the provider of services, for example, the hospital, sends the claims to Medicare which pays the hospital directly. You only have to sign the claim form to verify that you received the stated services.

For Part B, if your doctor accepts the assignment, he or she files the claim and is paid directly by Medicare. If your doctor does not accept the assignment, you must file Form HCFA–1490S to receive reimbursement from Medicare. To make sure your claims are processed, file claims as soon as possible. Medicare allows you until December of the year following the year in which the charge was incurred to file. Beyond that date, claims will not be honored.

What Medicare does not cover

Below are some major items which Medicare will not pay for:

1. Custodial care that does not require the services of trained medical personnel. This includes care in a residential nursing home and help in preparing meals or getting around at home.

2. Preventive health care, such as annual checkups.

3. Glasses, contact lenses, and hearing aids and examinations to determine whether you need any of these items.

4. Cosmetic surgery.

5. Items considered personal comfort items rather than medical necessities, for example, a telephone in your hospital room.

6. The first three pints of blood needed during a hospital stay.

7. Most dental care.

8. Most foot care.

9. Injections that can be self-administered, such as insulin.

10. Generally, health care outside the United States.

Chapter 11
ESTATE PLANNING FOR RETIREMENT BENEFITS

RETIREMENT benefits may make up a sizable portion of your estate. Bank advertisements promise million-dollar funds for young workers who contribute the maximum amount annually to an IRA until retirement. Benefits from qualified pension or profit-sharing plans or Keogh plans will boost the amount. Benefits of key employees in closely held corporations may exceed $1 million from company plans alone. While it is impossible to figure the exact amount of your retirement benefits in 20 or 30 years, you should be able to project how much they would be if you died today, or in five years or ten years. If you are covered by a company plan, ask your plan administrator for some projections. Similarly, the trustee or custodian of your IRA can tell you your current holdings and how much they will be at the end of, say, your certificate term. Determining the size of the retirement fund will allow you to plan for its disposition and reduce the tax liability on the distribution.

How benefits from qualified plans are taxed

Distributions from qualified retirement plans are not taxed when:

1. The estate (including retirement benefits) reduced by deductible expenses is less than the estate tax floor; or
2. Benefits are paid to a surviving spouse; or
3. Payment is in the form of an annuity payable to a beneficiary other than your estate and the value of the annuity does not exceed $100,000. The value of the annuity above $100,000 is included in the gross estate. Benefits allocable to the cost factor of the annuity are not subject to tax; or

4. Payment is in a lump sum and the beneficiary (other than the estate) makes an income tax election to forgo the use of special ten-year averaging and capital gain treatment. If the election is made, up to $100,000 may be excluded from the gross estate.

EXAMPLES—

1. An individual dies in 1987 with a taxable estate of $550,000, including $150,000 of Keogh plan benefits. Since the estate is less than the $600,000 estate tax floor, there is no estate tax on the retirement benefits.

2. A man dies leaving his wife an estate of $2 million, including $500,000 in retirement benefits. Since the amount above the estate tax floor qualified for the marital deduction, there is no estate tax.

3. A woman with a substantial estate named her son as beneficiary of retirement benefits to be paid out as an annuity. The annuity was funded solely by her employer's deductible contributions. The value of the annuity up to $100,000 is excluded from the estate.

4. A father with a substantial estate named his daughter as the beneficiary of his retirement benefits which will be paid to her in a lump sum. The benefits are included in his estate and subject to tax unless the daughter elects not to use special ten-year averaging or capital gain treatment to report the distribution for income tax purposes. If the election is made, up to $100,000 passes tax free; the lump sum exceeding $100,000 is included in the father's estate. Whether it is advisable to make such an election is discussed later in this chapter.

Benefits which an employee is considered to have constructively received prior to death will be included in the estate whether or not the benefits are payable to the estate or to beneficiaries. Thus if a plan provides for a distribution of benefits at retirement and after retirement you continue to work but do not begin to take benefits, you are considered to have constructively received them unless you make an irrevocable election not to receive them until leaving the job. You should review your company plan to see if any potential constructive receipt problems exist and if they can be remedied.

With these rules in mind, here are some suggestions for naming recipients. You may want all or part of the benefits paid to your estate if the estate consists of substantial nonliquid assets and the benefits are needed to pay administrative costs and estate taxes.

If little or no estate tax is estimated, the decision to make benefits payable directly to beneficiaries or distributable through the estate may not be crucial unless you want to save administrative costs by having benefits pass outside the probate estate.

Should a beneficiary elect to forgo ten-year averaging?

A beneficiary receiving a lump-sum distribution may be reluctant to make the income tax election to forgo the use of special ten-year averaging or capital gain treatment if it requires the payment of more income tax than the combined estate tax and income tax due on the lump sum.

EXAMPLES—

1. Lump-sum benefits for a person dying in 1984 are $50,000. The estate is in the 37% bracket so the estate tax on the distribution is $18,500. Using ten-year averaging, the income tax is $2480. The combined tax on the distribution is $20,980. If the beneficiary is in the 50% income tax bracket and elects to forgo ten-year averaging, there is no estate tax on the sum but the income tax (after accounting for the $5000 death-benefit exclusion) is $22,500. Here the election is not advisable.

2. Same facts except the beneficiary is in a tax bracket lower than 50%. Here it may be advisable to make the election. For example, if the lump-sum distribution is the beneficiary's only taxable income, the income tax on it is only $11,789, or $8191 less than the combined estate tax and income tax using ten-year averaging.

If the estate is not subject to tax, even with the inclusion of lump-sum benefits, the beneficiary is always ahead with ten-year averaging. If the estate is in the 50% tax bracket, taxes will be reduced if the beneficiary elects to forgo ten-year averaging. To be sure of the most advantageous way to handle the election in your situation, compute the tax under alternative methods.

Individual retirement plans (IRAs)

As a practical matter, if the IRA owner dies before his or her entire interest has been distributed, the entire interest must, within five years from the date of death, be distributed or used to purchase an annuity for the beneficiary or beneficiaries for a term not exceeding their life expectancies and which will begin distributions immediately. However, if the owner had begun to receive distributions over a fixed term, that term may be observed.

Over the course of your working career substantial IRA benefits may accumulate. However, up to $100,000 of retirement benefits, including IRA benefits, may escape estate tax.

If benefits are payable to your spouse it does not matter how payment is made; while benefits will be included in the estate, they will not be taxed because of the marital deduction. However, income tax consequences may determine your spouse's choice of payment method since all IRA benefits are taxed as ordinary income when received.

If benefits are paid to your estate, they are included in your estate and subject to tax. Benefits are not included in your estate if paid to a beneficiary as an annuity contract or other arrangement in which a series of substantially equal payments are made for the life of the beneficiary or over a period ending at least 36 months after your death. The exclusion is subject to this limitation: up to $100,000 of the aggregate of retirement benefits (e.g., benefits from corporate plans and IRAs) is excludable. Payments are not considered substantially equal if the amounts payable during any 12-month period exceeded 40% of the total benefits payable (as determined on the date of your death). When the beneficiary is given an option to take periodic payments or payments at other intervals, benefits will be excluded only if periodic payments are elected no later than the date the estate tax return is filed. The election is made by filing an election with the IRA trustee or custodian requiring the trustee or custodian to pay out the proceeds as an annuity over at least three years or use the funds to buy an annuity contract (payable over at least three years) from an insurance company. The election is irrevocable.

If a person made excess contributions to an IRA that were not corrected prior to death, a portion of the benefits is included in the estate. The excludable portion is determined according to a special formula contained in proposed Treasury regulations.

Benefits from IRA rollover accounts are treated in the same manner as IRAs, provided that the initial rollover was from a qualifying plan, such as a retirement annuity purchased by an exempt organization.

IRAs of nonworking spouses. IRAs of nonworking spouses are treated in the same manner as regular IRAs. If benefits are payable to other than the nonworking spouse's estate, the beneficiary should ascertain whether an election to take periodic benefits is possible in order to avoid estate tax on the benefits.

Estate tax treatment of beneficiary. The estate of the employee is not taxed on the IRA if the above conditions are met. However, when the beneficiary of that IRA dies before the account is exhausted, the beneficiary's estate may not escape tax. If the beneficiary made a rollover of the deceased employee's IRA, but made no other contributions, the entire account is included in the beneficiary's estate. If the beneficiary made a rollover and also made contributions on his or her behalf, then the portion of the account attributable to the beneficiary's own contributions may be excluded.

How death benefits under nonqualified plans are taxed

Employers may offer plans, such as deferred-compensation plans, permanent disability benefits, and unfunded survivor's benefit plans, to pay benefits on an employee's death. Here are guidelines for determining whether benefits to which your survivors may be entitled will be taxable.

Benefits are included in the employee's estate under these circumstances:

1. The employee had the right under the contract or plan to name or change the beneficiaries, or to change the amounts payable to the beneficiaries.

2. The employee had the right to receive an annuity or other payment (alone or with another person, such as a spouse) for his or her life or for a stated number of years or for any period which does not end before death under any form of contract or agreement. "Other" payments include only post-employment benefits.

3. The employee's estate has a contingent interest in the property in excess of 5% of its value. That is, the estate could receive more than 5% of the value of the benefits. For example, an employee arranged to have a fixed death benefit paid to his wife upon his death; if she predeceased him, the benefit was to be paid to his estate. Since his estate had a contingent interest in excess of 5% of the value of the death benefit (there was the possibility that the estate would receive 100% of the benefit in the event of the wife's premature death), it was includable in his estate.

Benefits are not included under these circumstances:

1. An employee has the right to temporary salary continuation under a sickness and accident plan.

2. Benefits are paid from life insurance in which the deceased had no incidents of ownership.

Treatment of special retirement benefits

Servicemen's survivorship annuities. The value of annuities for a surviving spouse and certain child beneficiaries under the Retired Serviceman's Family Protection Plan or the Survivor's Benefit Plan is excluded from the estate except to the extent of amounts deposited by a retired serviceman pursuant to Sections 1438 or 1452(d) of Title 10 of the U.S. Code.

Mine Safety Act benefits. A survivor's annuity under Title IV of the Coal Mine Health and Safety Act of 1969 is not included in the gross estate.

Railroad Retirement Act benefits. Lump-sum benefits under the Railroad Retirement Act are excluded if paid to a surviving spouse or parents under age 60. Surviving spouses and parents age 60 or older are entitled to other benefits under the act which are not excludable. Similarly, residual death benefits under Section 5(f)(2) of the act are includable if a decedent may designate beneficiaries.

Civil Service retirement benefits. The U.S. Civil Service Retirement System is considered a qualified pension plan. Thus benefits are included or excluded according to the rules discussed above.

⌐┛ The J. K. Lasser Tax Institute carries on the tax, financial, and business publications of J. K. Lasser. The Institute under the direction of Bernard Greisman continues the J. K. Lasser tradition of explaining complicated and technical material in terms understandable by the layman. It is also noted for its special tax services for professionals. The most widely read work for the public by the Institute is J. K. Lasser's Your Income Tax which has helped over 23 million taxpayers reduce taxes and make informed financial decisions.